Self help groups:
Getting started, keeping going

Judy Wilson
and
Jan Myers

R A Wilson, Nottingham

500245242

First edition published in 1986 by Longman
ISBN 0 582 89268 6

Second edition published in 1998 by R.A.Wilson,
38 Devon Drive, Sherwood, Nottingham NG5 2EN

British Library Cataloguing in Publication Data

Wilson, Judy, 1943 -
Self-help groups: getting started-keeping going. – 2nd ed.
1. Self-help groups
I. Title   II. Myers, Jan
361.7

ISBN 1 874259 00 3 2nd revised edition

Cover design by Tony Marson, 4 Sheets Design & Print, Nottingham

Typeset in 10 point Palatino by Jim McLean, Nottingham.

Printed and bound in Great Britain by Antony Rowe,
Chippenham, Wiltshire.

Contents

Foreword

by Professor KCMM Alberti,
President, Royal College of Physicians

Over the past few years self help groups have blossomed for a whole range of diseases and disorders. This is most welcome and represents a paradigm shift in medical thinking.

Physicians are increasingly recognising that people feel they need more than just professional help, particularly social support and ways of diminishing the common feeling of being alone. Meeting other people in similar situations can offer new knowledge and perspectives.

It is also recognised that management of medical conditions, particularly chronic diseases, is a co-operative task involving the person with the condition, their family, the doctor and, often many other health professionals. Taking part in a self help group can help people feel more confident about working with health professionals.

The mutual support offered by self help groups means that people both give and receive support. Helping other people in a similar situation can itself be very helpful.

This new edition of this very practical handbook, which does just this, is to be welcomed. It will give help and succour to many. We owe a great debt to Judy Wilson and her colleagues.

Introduction

Starting and running self help groups is like going on a journey. The places you pass through, the route you take, the way you travel and the people you go with – these are your decisions. Written primarily for people thinking of starting or running their own groups, this book covers some of the more significant stops on the journey. It will also be useful to paid workers or volunteers working to support self help initiatives.

Self-help is a way of tackling lots of issues in life, and lies behind many community groups. Here we are talking to people in a particular kind of self-help group: one based on a sharing a personal situation. It could concern health, a serious illness or a disability. It could be a personal situation that leaves you feeling isolated and uncertain, or some sudden impact in your life, like bereavement, may have left you wanting to get together with people who've gone through it too. This guide may be useful to people in other self help groups, but it's aimed at people in this particular sort of group – perhaps "mutual support groups" is a better way of describing them. They are groups which cover mental and physical health, social issues, disability and carers groups. The book first looks at what is meant by self help. Although joining a group is part of a journey of self discovery, it is much more about working with others to achieve common goals – the process of mutual support. But the important thing about self help groups is that they are made up of people who set out to help themselves and other people who share the same situation or condition.

The book also covers many issues that are common to all kinds of groups, and some that are special to groups in the health field:

starting a group, attracting and keeping members, how groups work, and how they relate to each other, to the community they are in, and to the professionals who work with their members. The final chapters look at how they change, how to end them (something most handbooks ignore!), and how their members can see whether they are doing the right job.

Self help groups are not presented as a panacea. They may not be appropriate for everyone or every situation. Joining or starting one needs a good deal of thought, commitment and often hard work. It is helpful to begin with a blend of belief in self help and its enormous benefits, mixed with realism, caution and an awareness of the difficulties involved.

Throughout the book, you will find real life examples from existing self help groups and their members. At the back of the book are lists of useful addresses, books and training materials geared to helping you to find out more information, to put you in touch with local sources of support and to help you to continue on your journey long after you have put this book down.

1   What *is* a self help group?

We are all likely to be affected, at sometime in our lives, by ill-health, caring for a friend or relative, physical disability, despair, loneliness or the feeling of being isolated and alone. Finding someone with whom we can share our experience, a person who may be facing a similar situation, can often provide comfort and relief. Through mutual understanding and support, members of self help groups share their knowledge and expertise in coping, increase their learning and understanding, and make personal changes in their lifestyle.

Definition of a self help group

A self help or mutual aid group consists of people who have personal experiences of a similar problem or life situation, either directly or through their family or friends. Sharing experiences enables them to give each other a unique quality of mutual support and to pool practical information and ways of coping. Groups are run by and for their members.

Some self help groups expand their activities: they may provide, for example, services for people who face a similar problem or life situation; they may campaign for change. Professionals may take part in the group in various ways, when asked to by the group.

Some groups will hold regular meetings on a weekly, monthly or quarterly basis. Meetings may be in public venues, such as community centres, or in members' homes. Other groups will maintain support through letter writing, through a network of telephone contacts or through usenet groups or e-mail.

(Self Help Nottingham, 1997; extract)

Key principles

People in self help groups join together because of the common life circumstances in which they find themselves – for example, coping with bereavement, living with a family member with drink or drug related problems, or trying to find someone who may also have a child with the same illness.

The common bond experienced by members of a mutual support group is more than a shared interest which may be found, for example, in a rose growers' association or a bowls club. Here people join a club because they want to be involved in an activity they enjoy. They may find that through shared activity they make friends with people with whom they can share very personal matters and worries. In a self help group the bond is the condition, situation or problem they share. Of course from that may grow friendships and shared activities. Self help groups are also places for fun and laughter.

Another key principle is that people in groups should take on some responsibility for coping with their own problem.

> "I had a lot of help from the doctors, from my family and the church", Janet said when talking about her reaction to having cancer diagnosed. "But I felt I had to do something for myself too."

People in self help groups are prepared to do something for themselves. It may well be in addition to professional care or it may be because they are seeking an alternative to the health and social services on offer. Each person has a sense of owning or owning up to an issue, for example "My name is Philip and I'm an alcoholic . . . " may be the best known of introductions at a twelve steps meeting for Alcoholics Anonymous.

People probably go to and form groups for a variety of reasons but initially most people go to self help groups to meet their own needs.

In this sense, "self" is about self awareness and self determination. However, much of the benefit of groups comes from helping each other; of being able to help and of being helped. Many people find that the support they also give to other members of the group helps them too.

> Jane, a member of a widows' group, went to get help for herself but added, "It helped me get over my own bereavement when I suddenly found I was being useful to other people."

These feelings of well being, self esteem, being in control of your situation, finding and giving information and support are experienced most when the group is working well together. Self help groups are based on principles of sharing and working co-operatively. In this context, self help is probably more accurately described as mutual aid or mutual support.

> "There's a strength you can get from others. People in groups want to work together, not just tackle their problem on their own." Margaret was quite overwhelmed with the support she immediately got from being part of a group facing the same problem, anorexia.

Some people join or start self help groups because they have been through a similar experience and wish to support others who are now facing that task. Some wish to establish an identity other than "a patient with epilepsy" or "a client with mental health problems". Others may say they need a label in order to get help from professional services.

> For a number of years Mary had been aware that her young son was not like other children of his age. His behaviour was sometimes erratic and he had difficulty in coordinating his movements. For a long time, no-one could determine what the matter was. Eventually, Mary was told that her son had dyspraxia. She had no idea what this was and was determined to learn more about it. She went to the library and read as much as she could, formed a local self help group to meet others and made contact with the national organisation. At last, Mary had something to pin her concern upon and she was able to discuss therapy and special education needs with professionals because her son was dyspraxic.

Perhaps the most important of the key principles underlying self help groups is that groups are run by and for their members, that is, the person facing the issues, or their family or friends, or both.

"We felt we wanted to take responsibility for the group ourselves ...
It was difficult to do it all, but important that people didn't do good
to us ... " Pete and Sue, both with severe physical disabilities.

Self help groups can be seen as part of a continuum where professionally-led therapy or support groups form one end point and self help groups form the other. This does not mean that professionals and volunteers cannot be useful to self help groups, but group members are right to see the group as theirs and to decide on the membership and activities.

Self help
groups

Professionally led
groups

It is worth also remembering that self help groups do not replace medical or social care. Self help groups are one way in which people exercise their responsibilities for themselves and for other people. They are not a substitute for public services or private care. The information and support they provide is something different, valuable in its own right.

Self help groups vary in size. Very often the size can be determined by the type of activity of the group. If a group aims to provide mutual support through discussion, sharing experiences and coping techniques, this will not easily be achieved with 80 people attending meetings. The rest of the book is about how to make groups work, but before moving on to the next chapter, Starting a Group, there may be several questions and tasks you may wish to think about.

Joining a group or starting one

Self help groups are not always very visible – there might well be a group in your area already in operation. If it gives you what you want, then you may decide to join it and put your energies and time into being a member of an existing group, rather than into setting up a new one. Or you may still decide to go ahead and start your own.

Do you want to start a group?

Have you got some spare time?

You may not need a lot, but you should have some space in your life in the coming, say, 12 months.

What do members of your family and close friends think?

Can you cope with intrusion into your home, by people or the telephone?

Can you face other people's problems as well as your own?

Are you well enough? – at least sometimes.

Are you mobile? It need not stop you starting a group, but you'll need to think through the implications.

Have you got a telephone? This needn't stop you either, but you'll need to think of ways of managing without one.

Can you cope with the challenge? It need not all depend on you, but a group will make demands on you: emotional, financial and physical.

Think of all the positive results that could come from starting a self help group. Your life might change completely. You're more than likely to get at least some help with your own problem. You'll make new friends. You may get busy and fulfilled. And you may discover talents and skills within yourself you never dreamt you had.

So think about joining an established group as an option. It may in fact suit you more than starting a new one. First though, find your self help group. Be prepared for a bit of detective work.

In some areas of the country there are now local support and information centres or support workers especially for self help groups. If you have one of these, you will not only get information but extensive help and advice, geared specially for you.

There may be a national organisation who can tell you if they have a local branch or contact in your area. Your local library will probably have such a directory, which will give details of established national self help organisations.

Other possible sources of information are the Freephone Health Information Service (0800 665544), the Council for Voluntary Service, the Citizens Advice Bureau, the disability help line DIAL, health centres, the local council information department, doctors, nurses, community nurses and health visitors, social workers and the local newspaper or radio station.

Even the most exhaustive detective work may not result in your finding an established group. Or you may find one, and decide you still want to go ahead and form your own. In either case, you'll probably have picked up some useful information, contacts and possible resources on the way, so the detection exercise won't have been wasted. So what's the next step?

Stop and think whether you really want to start a group. Don't worry about if you will be able to, but ask yourself if you really want to. Don't underestimate yourself. Even if you've never done anything like this before, you'll be surprised at what you are capable of achieving.

So, stop and weigh it up. Think of the year ahead and whether you can put your energy and commitment into a group for that length of time. If you can't, then it may be better to shelve the idea – for good, or maybe until your life or other circumstances change.

Remember that the group won't be just you, of course – it will be several people working together.

2 Starting a group

By this time you may have visited one or more self help groups to find out what they are like, what ideas you can get from their experience and what pitfalls to avoid. You may have discussed the idea with friends and family. Maybe you were encouraged in this venture by a colleague or health professional you have been able to use as a sounding board on what to do next. You may or may not, at this point, have found like-minded people to join you, or an organisation which can give practical help or support such as a self help centre or local Council for Voluntary Service. So what do you do next?

Think about the type of group you wish to set up

Liz was already a member of a organisation based on a common problem, diabetes. It ran, though, as a rather formal voluntary organisation and only met infrequently. Liz wanted a small, mutual support group, meeting more often to help her cope with everyday living. Her job had given her experience, and confidence in organising, but she was anxious about whether she could manage time for a group. What about her health? What did her family think? Would the group all come to depend on her? She took thinking time over several months and emerged with the support of her family and a realistic commitment of her time and energy.

There are many different kinds of groups and ways of running groups. Some groups are very informal with small numbers of people who may take turns in organising or running the group. Some groups are just for people who are carers, some people choose to have carers in the same group as the people on the receiving end of that care. Some groups have a certain number of members and then operate as a closed group until they need to recruit new members. Others have an open membership where people can come and go. Some larger groups choose to operate on a more formal basis with a committee and officers such as chair, secretary and treasurer. Some groups have links with health and social services and closely complement their services. Others set up in answer to perceived gaps in services. Some have a loose organisational structure, while others, such as the "twelve-step" groups like Alcoholics Anonymous, have a definite way of running their groups and behaviour codes for members.

Until you decide what you want the group to achieve you may not be able to decide on the structure best suited to help you to do this. If the issue is a rare health condition, it may not be possible to meet face to face and you may need to explore other methods of meeting.

The purpose and structure of the group may also change over time and as members join or leave the group. It is important to be aware that these types of change may occur. They affect what happens within the group – how you relate to each other and how you carry out your aims. They also affect how you and others view the group and if it meets your needs. A self help group cannot be a one-person show, however energetic or experienced that person may be. It is a positive coming together of several people with the same problem. While you do need to make a personal commitment, it is best to try to bring others on board. You can start a group with two people but four or five is a good number to begin planning and gives a stronger base to discuss ideas, goals and objectives.

Find some like-minded people

Jenny had several members in her immediate family who suffered from severe asthma. She needed information and support herself and had ideas on useful activities for asthma sufferers. She located a local asthma group and travelled over to the south side of the city to go to its daytime meetings. It was a positive, helpful group, but it didn't meet all Jenny's needs. She wanted something more local, evening meetings and activities such as swimming. She discussed the idea of a new group in the north of the city with the group in the south, and went away with their support and possible plans for occasional joint meetings.

Some groups, like the asthma group, are part of larger national associations. The national associations may be able to help you to set up a local branch, they may be able to put people living in the vicinity in touch with you. Or, as in this case, an existing local branch may be able to give help and advice in establishing another local group.

You may also need to look for people who are in a similar position to yourself. A group of parents of pre-school children with special needs, for example, may have more in common with each other – even if the needs are different – than with parents of teenagers.

This like-mindedness will apply not only to the common problem you are all facing, but to the general approach you have to tackling it. This may take some time – and some negotiation. A group which decides only to fund-raise for research or campaign for change is different from a group whose main object is mutual support, although they need not be mutually exclusive. Whatever your aim, make this clear when you are casting around for your first co-founders.

Janet was already quite ill by the time she decided to form a cancer group. It was essential for her to find other cancer sufferers who could work with her in setting up a group. She first found Ruth, through a local radio station's phone-in programme. Other like-minded people were put in touch with them through friends and through the Council for Voluntary Service, to form a first planning group.

How can you find your like-minded people? You will need to be very clear about who you are trying to attract – in this instance people to help to start a new group. Too much publicity too early can bring large numbers of potential members together too soon, before the group can cope and with expectations that a new group cannot meet. If you use posters or the local media you may need to think carefully about it.

Ideas for Publicity

Word of mouth – a good way of bringing people together.

Handwritten cards or notices in your local library, newsagent, corner shop, health food shop or book shop.

An advertisement in the personal column of the local paper, using a box number or a friendly organisation's address.

Supportive health and social service professionals.

A note in church magazines or weekly news-sheets.

A poster in a hospital outpatients' waiting area or a surgery or health centre – ask for their agreement first.

Use existing contacts that you may have already.

Each area will have its own opportunities and you can probably think of many others in your neighbourhood.

Get together

Pat and Richard were lucky. In their town, there was a self help groups support project that lent them a small room for their first planning meetings. Richard's main anxiety was his fear that a group would come to depend on him; Pat's that her home would be invaded. Both were suffering from migraine, an unpredictable condition that made their regular attendance questionable. Four small meetings were held over a three month period in which these problems were aired and they got to know each other. In particular, they spent a lot of time discussing the purpose of a group and the jobs to be done in setting it up.

All members of the initial group were emphatic that they didn't want to have sole responsibility and ways of sharing the jobs out was a topic that they looked at in depth.

Making time for careful planning can be very fruitful in helping a stable, effective group to emerge. What could you discuss in these informal meetings? You'll probably find you want to look at:

Membership: Is the group going to be just for people with the problem? Are their relatives welcome as well or do you in fact need two groups? Are you going to allow interested people or professional workers to come too, and how can you involve them without diverting the purpose of the group? How will potential members find out about you and how can they join? How can you control membership?

Size: Groups can vary from two to two hundred. Their size depends on many things, including how common the condition is and the objectives of the group. If you decide your main objective is mutual support through discussion, for example, then a membership of ten to twenty is probably reasonable. Don't be too ambitious about members, or get anxious if they appear to be few. Think about whether you want to restrict membership to a certain number – if you do what will you do if more people want to come. Will you operate a waiting list? How will it work?

Objectives: Self help groups can undertake all sorts of activities. What do you want out of the group at first? You'll find you need to think quite soon about what you want to do first and what you want to do in the long run.

By the time you have tackled these and other topics, you may find you have a group already, particularly if you decide on a small membership. In this case your next challenge is making it work, rather than going public. Often however, once people have talked through the issues in a small group, they decide to become more visible, go public and widen their membership.

Plan an initial meeting

While someone's front room may work well for planning meetings and for very small local groups, most groups will benefit from using a public building of some kind. It allows anonymity, a neutral base and flexibility, but you may need to consider other issues such as cost, availability, accessibility (both to the building and inside), size and comfort, amenities such as tea making facilities and adapted toilets for people using wheelchairs.

You will probably be most concerned to get a room quickly, and somewhere free. A Council for Voluntary Service, or a self help support team or worker, may very possibly be able to let you have a small, free room for a few sessions. Part of their job is to help people when starting up. If you need a larger room, health workers whom you know may be able to arrange a room in a hospital or health service building. Other organisations, especially if you have a personal contact, may also be worth approaching.

You will also need to consider the time of year. It's amazing how a combination of holiday periods and bad weather can restrict the available months: spring, early summer and early autumn are generally good times for a launch. Time of day, and day of the week need to be considered too. Think too about local cultural or religious festivals or special sporting events and other activities which may stop people from attending.

You'll need to think carefully about the type of meeting you want to hold. Will it be a small informal meeting for new people to get to know each other? Or a larger meeting with a well-known local or national speaker to try to attract a larger number of people some of whom may be interested in joining your new group? At the same time as organising the first meeting, start thinking in your planning group about a second. If the first one is successful, people will want to know, on the spot, when they can meet again. It's worth guessing among you what might be an acceptable date and place, and making a provisional booking of the same, or another room.

Whether it is a large or small meeting there are the same questions to answer and jobs to allocate. Who will make sure the room is booked and open on time? Will people need signs to direct them to your meeting place, or from the meeting room to the toilets, car park etc.? Will someone greet people as they arrive? What will people do with their coats? Who will organise refreshments and when will they be made available? Will they be free or will you make a charge? Will you ask for names and addresses of all people attending ? Will someone be on hand to talk to people during and after the meeting? How will people recognise that person? Will you ask people to introduce themselves? Do you want one person to talk about why you organised the meeting?

And the questions go on. It may be useful to spend time recording these and other questions on a big sheet of paper as they occur to you. They can then be used as a checklist. If you have time to think through these issues and prepare before the first meeting, the easier it will be for you to relax and cope with anything that occurs at the meeting itself.

3 Membership, Purpose and Participation

It is for the group to decide who can belong to it.

> Supertwins was a group for parents of triplets, quads, etc. The triplets were going with their father to a party arranged by the group. "Dad, why is it called Supertwins?" one asked. He explained. The child thought for a moment and said, "We only just made it, didn't we?"

The more specific you can be about membership, and the more precise about the group's purpose, the more likely it is to succeed, so it's worth giving ample time to thinking about and discussing both. You can use different people as sounding boards and draw from the experience of other groups. Decisions about activities will then emerge more easily.

Who can belong to the group?

You may have taken some decisions already in your search for a few like-minded people. You may want the group to be open to anyone in your area who shares your condition – or even anyone in the country, if you have a rare condition. You may have to go to some trouble to make sure that it really is open to all.

For example, if the membership of your group is for all people living in a certain area with diabetes, you need to think about how you reach all the different communities living in that area so that they have equal access and opportunity to become members. It may not be enough to say "our group is open to all". You need special publicity or special help with contacts to reach, say, younger people, or people for whom English is a second language. You must make sure that the way people get to know about the group, and the way it works, attracts them and doesn't put them off.

You must make very sure you do not exclude anyone on grounds of race or ethnic origin, and that the way your group is run does not make it unwelcoming, say to men, or to women, or to younger or older people.

Even completely open groups will be for people who share the same need or condition, and there will be some understanding about how wide an area the group serves, and perhaps how big it may become.

Groups with restricted membership ─────────

However, from the very first you may have taken a decision that restricts the membership of the group. For example, you may personally be sure that you only want to get together with people who have direct experience of your problem. This means you will not be inviting either your relatives or other people's families to become members of the group. You have decided who can join, and this means some people are excluded. Don't feel guilty about this. Some of the most successful groups are those who are very specific about who can join.

There are many groups which are organised around age, race and gender or some special circumstance to meet the needs of their members. Here are some examples.

- Women surviving incest and sexual assault – where the perpetrators have been male and women would not feel safe sharing a meeting space with men

- A divorced Asian women's group – meeting the particular cultural needs of women in this situation and where Asian women are under-represented in other groups for divorced people

- Young people with arthritis – where the needs of young people under a certain age are seen as different from those of older people with arthritis

- A group for young black graduates – to provide mentors and support for young professionals moving from their experience of university into the world of work

- A group whose members need to belong to a small group, which therefore limits its numbers

It may not always be appropriate for the boundaries of membership to be drawn too tightly. Often people feel that attending a group with their partner is one way of understanding and coming to terms with their problem together. Sometimes whole families, for example those with one child who has a physical disability and others who are able bodied, may get immense benefit from attending.

There are other patterns. You may even decide that you will set up two groups running side by side, one of which will be for carers. They might meet independently for mutual support and come together for larger meetings where a speaker might be invited, or for information exchange.

For some groups special conditions exist ————

Carers' groups are formed by the people caring for a relative or friend with a disabling disease like Alzheimer's Disease and will naturally be restricted to them. One particular feature of carers' groups is that people don't always get told a group exists – they are not the patients. And yet by others they are often seen only in relation to the patients:

> "The first question most people ask you when they met you in the street is how's your mum, or your auntie or your husband. They don't ask after you."

Physical illnesses such as sickle cell anaemia have a high profile among black communities and have been taken up by self help groups nationally. Because of the "real experience of racism" (F.Agbalaye), black people do not always seek out or obtain services, and it may be very important to meet with other black people "to meet and discuss in private the issues that concern them, without fear of disbelief or ridicule". There are other groups which have been set up because of particular needs, e.g. for mixed race parents.

There are also groups for people where the condition or situation is such that special conditions of confidentiality and privacy are necessary, and the group may strictly control access to it.

This is a general rule: all groups limit their membership in some way or other. This must be for a good reason – the shared condition, or because they need to stay small, or the special circumstances of the members. If it is an open group, it must be genuinely open to all who qualify for membership.

What do you want to achieve?

You may think this is self-evident once you have decided on membership. A common bond brings you together so you will all have the same ideas about what the group is for and what you want to achieve. It's all too easy though for people to assume there is agreement over what the group is about, and to coast along without being clear what you are trying to do. Being specific can definitely contribute to success. You need to decide what the goals, objectives and priorities of the group are to be. You will also need to ask questions about what you aim to achieve at regular intervals. Your experience as the group changes and the change in the environment in which you are working will influence what you do, how and when.

Who decides on the goals?

Decisions on goals, objectives, priorities and membership could be made by group leaders. They could simply tell the members of the group what is going to be done. But you must start as you mean to go on, and involve all the members of the group in deciding the goal, objectives and priorities from the beginning. This may be done in one or two informal meetings. With a group that is going to be larger, it may mean some members working together, perhaps even consulting outside with a self help worker or other professionals, and bringing their conclusions back to a structured meeting of all the members. But it is the members who must make the decision.

Deciding your goals and objectives

Goals or aims are the main purposes of the group – and every group member should have the opportunity to determine these. Even if groups in different towns share the same problem, the goals they set themselves maybe very different. If you are setting up a local branch of a national organisation, however, you may need to take on their goals in order to qualify for affiliation. National organisations are often very definite about goals for local branches.

When thinking about the overall goal try to set out in one or two sentences a broad description of what your group is about and the difference you want to make. For example, a group might begin with the statement:

> "To overcome the isolation felt by people caring for a loved one with dementia and to make sure they can get information, support and appropriate care and services"

You might want to include a statement about your values. You may want to emphasise that group members need to share responsibility, and respect each other's individual views. The group might extend its statement:

> "To overcome the isolation felt by people caring for a loved one with dementia and make sure they can get information, support and appropriate care and services in ways which respect people's individual needs and choices"

Once you have agreed your overall goal and values, you can start to think of what you have to do in order to make it real. You set goals which are more specific about what you will achieve. The group in our example might want to describe its specific goals as:

– To give all carers of people with dementia in this city a chance to meet and make contact

- To increase the awareness of rights and access to benefits and services for carers

- To develop self-confidence in helping carers cope

Objectives are the smaller and more precise targets the group sets itself in order to achieve its goals. You are unlikely to be able to work on them all at once, so you will need to set priorities. It is possible to look at the activities you want to do immediately, what you think you might be able to carry out in two years time and even consider longer term developments. For example, the objectives might be:

- To organise a self help group meeting once a month for members

- To provide a helpline for carers

- To run a welfare rights information day twice a year

It may take time to agree goals and objectives but these will form the basis of your group so it is worth taking your time. It may be that as a group you are able to organise regular self help group meetings right away and you may have a supportive professional welfare rights worker willing to give their time every so often so you can feel confident of providing this service to your members.

A service like a helpline or an information session may clash with other aims of the group, or completely change its nature. Such a change may come later. Membership of the group can be small in order to achieve an effective self help group, but may need to grow in order to build up numbers of people for both a group and a service like a helpline. When you make this kind of decision you are setting priorities.

A new group in a country area decided that mutual support through talking was high on their list of priorities. Ideally, they would have liked to meet frequently but transport and lack of a central meeting place made this difficult. But they found that everyone was on the phone. They decided to set up a system for phone contact, and for letter writing to complement occasional meetings.

A group taking this sort of approach is being realistic. When you consider what activities you could undertake, think realistically, concentrating on what is feasible, and what strategies you could adopt to help you achieve your aims. Ask yourselves:

– What is right for us?

– What is feasible?

– How fast can we move?

Attracting and keeping members

So the search for members may be determined by what you wish to do. How you determine membership can also affect what you do too. If you count every person who rings the contact telephone number or comes to one meeting, you may find that over time your membership grows. Although there may be dozens of members, perhaps only a few are active members – regularly coming to meetings and taking part in organised events. Not every person can come to meetings because of lack of transport or other difficulties so you need to think about membership quite carefully. On the one hand do not exclude anyone for no good reason. But do not cause unnecessary problems for the group. For example, if you have many inactive members, and decide to register as a charity or have a formal constitution which requires a minimum attendance at meetings in order to make decisions, then the group may not be able to function.

Some groups ask people to try and build in a commitment to attendance. It is wise however to be relaxed about this, especially as so many people will have problems that make regular attendance uncertain. Most groups have an open door policy, and accept that many people will come in and out. But bear in mind that many of the more established groups have a hard core of regular attenders. This can be an important element in the success of a self help group, though it takes time to achieve.

Some groups get round this by having different kinds of members. There may be some people who cannot or do not want to attend meetings but who want to be kept in touch with what the group is doing. Some groups charge a subscription whereby in exchange for a certain amount a year, people can receive newsletters and invitations to public meetings or fund-raising events. In this way, the groups are starting to think about how they can help people to participate in ways which are comfortable and appropriate for them. Sometimes, it can be that the small core of regular attenders is overwhelmed by the task of trying to keep a growing number of people informed by organising events and newsletters. In this instance, it may be useful to step back to look at what is being done and whether or not it still meets people's needs; it may be that circumstances have changed and people who dropped out of the group could be encouraged to return if they were made aware of the changes. There are a number of methods to help you to do this kind of activity. One is to send a questionnaire to all the people on your list to ask them what they want from the group, what they might be able to offer and what would encourage them to attend.

This kind of exercise can also highlight different ways in which people can participate – for example one person may not be able to attend meetings but would be very willing to make cakes for a coffee morning; another person may be able to help out with organising social events if they knew they didn't have to do it on their own. There's no reason why one person has to do one job – look at the jobs that need to be done in your group. Can they be broken down into smaller tasks so that more people can participate?

Tasks of a group secretary

>   Minute taker
>
>   Letter writer
>
>   Membership record-keeper
>
>   Room booker
>
>   Agenda and minutes distributor

We have already started to identify five jobs which could be done by five different people. To take this further, you could even think of having a membership group. Here you could have several people taking on several different tasks: welcoming new members to the group, acting as telephone contacts for the group, keeping subscriptions up to date and so on.

Membership and participation is a vital feature of any group and the areas where most problems occur. People need to gain something from being part of a group – they come of their own free will and it needs to be a positive and fulfilling experience in order that people will keep coming. The benefits of membership of self help groups are most felt when people are able to put as much into a group as they take out. This means taking account of the natural ups and downs a group may experience. People may not always be well, and it may be harder for them to play a full part. It may mean thinking wider than the boundaries of a monthly group meeting, for example using telephone calls or social meetings, to help people to join in. Participation is not just about handing out jobs, it is also about opportunities to communicate, to share, to feel a sense of belonging to and ownership of the group.

4   Communication:
how groups work

Creating good communication ──────────

Communication is important because:

-   It improves contact between people in groups.

-   It allows members to understand what is going on.

-   It gives people the opportunity to participate in ways
    appropriate to their needs and those of others.

Personal support will probably evolve naturally in your group
meetings, in friendships outside the group and in telephone calls
between group meetings. Often it needs to be worked at.

What especially affects communication in self help groups?

Size makes a lot of difference. A group with a membership of
fifteen or less will be rather different to that of over fifteen. Really
big numbers bring other challenges.

It's wise to assume you'll have some turnover, so plan communication to meet the needs of existing and new members.

The problem facing members will influence the way you communicate. In particular, if people have any hearing loss, visual
impairment or problems with speech, you'll need to think
through together how people can participate.

How well do you communicate?

How many members do you know by name?

How many names do new members know?

How do people find out about special activities?

How do new members find out about earlier decisions made by the group?

If someone has a new idea, how do they put it forward?

How, if at all, do members communicate outside meetings?

How do new members find out about contact outside meetings?

Is there an informal part to your meeting for one-to-one chat?

Does the room where you meet help or hinder communication?

Is there time in your meetings to discuss arrangements and future plans?

Do people trust each other?.

Are discussions confidential?

How do you cope with distressing situations in your group?

How do you handle conflict?

The structure of the group, and of the meetings, will affect how well you communicate and what methods you use. Groups who meet infrequently, for example, may put more emphasis on telephone links and newsletters. Groups who form a committee will need to consider how the committee communicates with the rest of the group.

A feeling of equality among members makes communication easier. If certain people dominate discussions, new members or people uncertain of themselves will hesitate to join in. Communication will be easier in groups where everyone feels they have

Ground rules agreed by self help group members on a course

Confidentiality

No Smoking

The right to stand back and not join in

Have fun

Be supportive

Considerate

Understanding

Encouraging

Non-judgmental

Not to make assumptions

Ask questions and clarify

Start and finish on time

Let people finish speaking

Don't generalise

Respect ourselves and each other

No competition in learning and experience

Be honest and sincere

Constructive criticism – putting things positively

Sharing experiences

Time to ourselves

Genuineness

something to contribute, and are encouraged to do so. However, just because someone is quiet in the group, it does not necessarily mean they are not participating. It may be quite a while before someone decides to join in. They may learn about the group and its members by watching and listening.

Communication is not only about how messages are passed between members but how people learn about each other; how they learn to support and comfort each other in appropriate ways and about being open and flexible enough to be able to raise questions, ideas, resolve conflicts. It is about finding out if someone is upset whether they like to be left alone, or if they appreciate it if someone sits closely by or holds their hand. Communication is therefore on both an individual and a group level. It is about trust and about confidentiality within the group.

Often groups will sit together in their early stages and agree some basic ideas, or ground rules, which help to make each person feel safe in the group. Members can start to agree what is appropriate for the group and what might be thought inappropriate behaviour. Yelling and swearing at someone might be seen as unacceptable, yet showing anger may be appropriate in some circumstances.

These rules can also give a foundation for reviewing how effective the group is at communicating. Like all rules, they are not set in stone and changes can be negotiated within the group.

It is important to record ideas and decisions made by the group so that they are not lost. This can be done in the form of minutes taken at each meeting. There are other ways to create a history for the group too – creating a scrap book or diary of significant events, photographs, press cuttings and thank you letters.

Groups go through different stages of development and different aspects of communication and actions occur within and across the group. Often in the initial stages of setting up, when people are just getting to know each other, they are polite and reticent about challenging ideas put forward by another.

Conflict and difficulties

As people settle in and form their own ideas of what the group is about and how it should be run, then disagreements occur, and in-fighting can take place. Sometimes there is such disagreement, especially in small groups, that the group does not survive; or members separate to follow their own ideas. However, if the group does emerge through this stage then its members usually start to redefine what the group is about, its goals, objectives, membership and activities.

When people start out, they do not imagine that they will ever be in conflict with others in the group and they may not therefore take the time to discuss thoroughly goals, objectives, structure etc. Only when there is upset do they concentrate their minds on setting guidelines. Often many areas of conflict can be due to lack of communication between members – one person may still be struggling with the fundamental function of the group and another may be trying to organise fund-raising or publicity activities. Conflict can occur if one seems to be blocking the other and this behaviour can be interpreted by both in a number of ways – arrogance, stubbornness, insensitivity. By allowing the two points of view to be communicated, there may be common ground on which to bring the two together. It may mean stepping back from the rush of activity to review goals and direction and setting a pace suited to all members. Once a group can resolve issues such as this, then it is probably at its most effective.

Development is not a process which groups pass through stage by stage in a straight line. Some groups can miss stages, or by a sudden turn of events an effective group may find itself facing profound difficulties. This can happen where groups look on the surface as if they are effective, dynamic groups. Close observation reveals that most of the decision making or direction is being led or promoted by one key figure. Where there is no real dialogue within the group and no real sharing of responsibility, and that person were suddenly to leave, the group would find itself struggling to survive. An equally strong figure taking up the reins, as " a saviour", would probably not solve the problem of lack of mutual support and responsibility.

Although groups sometimes need one or two people to take the group forward initially, in the long term good leadership makes it possible for other people to learn in the group, share responsibility and decisions, and work with each other. If this is achieved, then the effect of one person leaving the group is less. Jobs can be shared and in small groups decision-making is easier. In larger groups, especially those operating with a more formal structure involving committees and officer roles which carry status in the group, this needs more thought and more effort. Rotating membership of committees, or a limited number of years people can hold one post, are ways of getting people involved.

Having a democratic style of running a group does not mean that no one can make a decision on their own initiative. If the aims of the group are shared and accepted by all its members, then members given a job can feel empowered to act in the best interests of the group. They are aware of what the group would find acceptable and what would be detrimental to the group. And if the group formally appoints chair, secretary, treasurer and so on, their rights and duties should be clear.

> Kath has been secretary of her group for a number of years and wanted desperately to retire. For several meetings she had been asking if anyone might be interested in taking up the post. After one such meeting another member had a quiet word with her. Kath had been undoubtedly an excellent secretary and member of the group. However, in order to help the group she had often paid for postage out of her own money, had purchased stationery and didn't always ask for reimbursement for travel costs. Indirectly, this had affected how people perceived the job of secretary. They felt that if they did the job they would also have to behave in the same way. Kath was extremely grateful for this insight and once it was made clear that it was generally expected that members be reimbursed for appropriate expenses relating to the group, a volunteer came forward.

Getting the room right

Getting the right room for your meetings is very important. If it is a good place, you will find your meetings run much better, are more enjoyable and, most important, people are more likely to come.

A group needs an accessible and fairly stable base. If you need privacy, meeting in a coffee bar or a pub may make it hard for people to talk about their personal needs. Then again, so will a completely empty church hall with high echoing rooms, no heating and hard chairs!

The furnishing, and various little touches also make a difference – ash trays if smoking is allowed (and if not, is there a break for people who want to smoke?), or boxes of tissues, biscuits or flowers.

You may be offered free use of a room which you may find suitable for your early meetings but if it is connected to a hospital or psychiatric unit, it may put people off attending – they may regard it merely as an extension of professional services. Likewise, meeting in someone's home can indicate to a new member that the group is cosy and filled with people who know each other and, perhaps quite wrongly, that newcomers will not be welcomed.

The Monday group welcomed the close link they had developed with hospital social workers, and the way it brought them new members. People were familiar with the hospital and there was much appreciation of the services it provided. The acceptance of the offer of a meeting room there seemed sensible. It brought problems however – a long walk from the entrance; poor sign-posting; uncertainty about exactly which room could be used; and no control about when the urn of coffee would arrive, if it did at all! The group decided to go for stability and continue to meet there. Some of the difficulties were resolved and they were careful to give good directions to new members.

The Thursday group's members had very mixed feelings about hospitals and consultants. Some had actually joined the group after despairing of professional care helping them at all. In no way could the group have met its objectives if it met on health service premises. A member's sitting room, central and with parking near, met their needs for the first year. But secretly the member began to resent using her flat and, as she got better, didn't always want to be at meetings herself. The solution was a comfortable informal room at a community centre, on a bus route, and with access to the kitchen to make drinks as and when they wanted. Small numbers sometimes meant that donations at the meeting didn't always cover the rent, but an occasional fund-raising event provided a subsidy.

Choosing a room

Here is a list of things to consider when you make a final decision about the kind of room you want for regular meetings.

Is the atmosphere welcoming?

Is the meeting place centrally located, within easy reach of the town, your neighbourhood or a group of villages?

Is the building easy to find from the street?
Will you need to send a map?

Is the room easily identifiable when you get in the building?

Can you put up notices about your meeting?

Is the room accessible for anyone with a physical disability? (Think about this even if your group is not based on a physical disability). Are there toilets and ramps for disabled people?

Is there a loop system for people with hearing loss?

Is the meeting place near a public transport route?

Is there parking? Is it near enough the entrance for people with a disability?

Will the room seat the number of people you expect?

What time of day, and which day of the week is best?

Is there room for any activities? (e.g. small discussion groups).

Are the chairs all the same height? (it helps discussion if they are).

Are the chairs suitable? (e.g. A young people's group may prefer cushions and a carpet; back pain sufferers will appreciate hard upright chairs).

Choosing a room (cont.)

Is there anything about the building or the room which could bring distress or difficulty to people, because of their personal problem?

Can you arrange the seating as you want?

Can you make, or get, tea and coffee at a time that suits you?

Is the building noisy? Or will it be when your meeting is held?

Is it warm? (More important than you might think.)

Do you need a board or flip chart?

Are you allowed to hold raffles?

What does it cost to hire?

Must you book a series of meetings in advance?

What are the caretaking arrangements?

What is the latest time by which you must leave?

The Wednesday group knew from the start that their problem meant that fund-raising would be difficult, especially as they had so many other things to do. They were keen to invite speakers on alternative therapies, operating outside the NHS. They had enjoyed joint meetings of self help groups held in a pleasant modern Social Services Day Centre for the elderly. The warden was anxious to see the building fully used, and negotiated a free letting for them too. The out-of-town location was balanced by good car parking and a most helpful caretaker.

A group for people with ME had been meeting in an upstairs meeting room provided by a self help centre for which they paid a small fee. Suddenly they had an influx of new members and the room was no longer big enough. Additionally, many of the members had mobility problems and found the stairs difficult. With the help of the centre, the group found a free meeting room with coffee making facilities and access for people with disabilities and car-parking in a social services centre which they could use in the evenings. It suited their needs perfectly.

Layout of the room

The layout of your room is very important for the success of your meetings.

You do not have to accept a room as the previous users left it (although you may have to leave it that way at the end of your meeting). Arriving early before the meeting starts gives you time to arrange the chairs the way the group needs them.

Most small groups find it is easier to share a problem or ideas if they sit in a circle, quite close to each other. Each member can see the others and can be aware of their actions and both verbal and non-verbal communication. Even if one or more persons facilitate the meeting, they will still be part of the circle of members.

One group for people with anxiety, stress and panic attacks meet in a small cosy room provided by a local self help centre. They are a small group and meet weekly. Before the meeting begins drinks are made. The room has comfortable chairs and the group make use of the two lamps for subdued lighting and to give the room a warm glow.

Tension and distress

Some groups play relaxation tapes or music to relax their members. Others are conscious of some members' need to sit by an open door. Others realise that some members will from time to time want to talk to someone away from the main group and try to make sure that a separate small room is available.

A group for incest survivors was meeting for the first time. Much planning had occurred over a number of months and each of the original members together with the self help development worker had a specific role to play in the meeting. Two people were specifically identified to the group for anyone who was distressed, needed to go out of the room and wanted someone to accompany them. One woman did feel the need to leave the meeting during the morning. A slight nod in the direction of one of the identified women was all that was needed. The meeting was able to continue and the woman was able to return and join in again a short time later.

Helping members to join in

Larger groups may have to be more creative in thinking how to help members participate. You may want to stay part of a larger group to listen to a speaker but for further discussion or for other activities you may want to consider breaking into smaller groups of three or four. This can also work when there is a lot of business to discuss. Work groups of interested people can look at issues such as fund-raising, publicity, or working out articles for the next newsletter for part of the meeting and report back their findings to the group as a whole for decision making. Leave time for informal mixing too. Sometimes groups try to do this over a cup of tea in a ten minute break but sometimes this can be the most beneficial part of the meeting and ten minutes may not be enough time. A balance has to be achieved between tasks and mutual support.

New members

Growth in membership helps members to change their role. As newcomers join the group, older members often feel more confident about the way they are coping. They begin to be a model for the newcomers, and have the opportunity to help others. This can often be as useful as receiving help. Groups have found that they are more effective if there are ways of old and new members sharing their experience. You can't leave this to chance: groups need to plan how this can be achieved in their particular setting. It is important to remember that first impressions hold a big impact and the first time a new person attends your meeting may well determine whether they come again.

Bill went to a group for carers of people with dementia accompanied by his son and after much persuasion. Although he found the meeting useful and the people helpful, welcoming and friendly, he felt totally overwhelmed by the whole situation. He would not have continued to go if his son had not accompanied him over the next four meetings. The turning point came when, after his wife was taken into a nursing home, he received a phone call from one of the regular members. He was able to talk over his feelings at a time when he felt most vulnerable and he has been an active member since that day. The group has learnt too. Now they have a welcoming group for new members.

Some groups have a particular person responsible for greeting new members; others operate a buddy type system where an existing member teams up with a newer member to introduce them to the group's other members and give a general feel for the group. Often they can meet people before a meeting and in between meetings.

Formality and informality

How your group is run is important. It needs to be formal enough to be well organised, but friendly enough to make new members feel welcome and involved. Getting the right balance between the two isn't always easy, but it can be done. There is no one way of organising a self help group, and your group will need to make its own decisions.

It may be tempting to drift along without any system of organising yourselves, but don't succumb to temptation. Groups do need some sort of structure – a framework is needed so that:

– Decisions are taken
– No one person dominates the group
– The group has stability and continuity
– New members understand what is going on
– New ideas can be introduced

It need not be complicated. Keep your structure simple. You can always add to a simple structure but it is much more difficult to take away from one which is over elaborate.

Like a number of anonymous groups, Depressives Anonymous (DA) has learnt a lot from Alcoholics Anonymous (AA). One particular local branch meets weekly – the meetings are the main source of support and has an attendance of 8–12. The group has evolved a pattern which is followed at each meeting, so anyone can act as chairperson. This job is shared around among most members. There is however a named treasurer who holds the job for a year and looks after the small amount of money that is involved. If there is some special piece of business to discuss – a change of meeting room for example – it's done in the whole group, convening a special meeting if necessary.

A Phobias Group set up with a "Trustees' Committee" and a formal constitution. The committee had responsibility for finance and for ensuring the group operated within the constitution. The group had difficulties. Members saw the need for more involvement in decision making and tasks by the whole group. They decided they needed better communication; creation of time and space for discussion; and flexibility over the contribution of each group member. They have now devised ways of achieving these while retaining the original framework.

What goes on at your meetings

At self help group meetings people receive information about services or the issue itself, companionship – the knowledge that they "are not the only one", practical advice and strategies for coping. Often other members can act as a model for newer, less experienced members in coping, for example, with deteriorating physical health. These are amongst the greatest benefits described by people who join self help groups and continue to go along to them. Some of the most common complaints are that there is not enough time to talk, that discussions can be dominated by one or two people – and that it is hard to retain new members and get people to join in. Bear these opinions in mind when you think how you want your group to work.

To summarise, your meetings are likely to be successful if you aim:

– to allow people time to talk
– to share information
– to make decisions about the group and to plan

- to help people to participate in ways in which they are comfortable
- to avoid one person monopolising the meeting
- to be aware of the needs of all members – new members and existing members

The size and purpose of your group will also affect the kind of meetings you run. You will need to ask:

- are there other pressures such as the need to fund-raise? How do you make links with other organisations? Do you expect funding from a public body so that you need to operate a bank account, book-keeping and other records?
- what's the ideal size for your group now and in the future?
- are you concentrating on mutual support, or running a variety of activities?

There are very few groups who do not have regular meetings – most people find they want this as a hard core of their activities, and for some groups, it is almost their only formal activity. Face to face contact, sharing in a group, making the effort to get out – these all seem to contribute to a self help group helping people with their problems.

Alcoholics Anonymous have evolved a particular way of running meetings. The twelve steps programme is a simple, but definite, structure to follow for each meeting and for the participation of each person within the group. Members have the chance to tell their story, and newcomers can take part as they want. It also means that each member can have the opportunity to chair the meeting.

A group for people who stammer found that a small informal grouping works best for them. It gives each person an opportunity to facilitate the meeting and also to get used to speaking in front of people in a supportive environment. They meet in a small meeting room with comfortable chairs in a circle. One person has responsibility for bringing the money tin to each meeting for members to contribute for refreshments and the hire of the room. Occasionally they invite a supportive speech therapist along to try out exercises and techniques.

A group for people who have cardiac impairment, some of which have had surgery meet monthly at a local hospital. Over 100 regular attenders enjoy a variety of speakers including cardiologists, paramedics, physiotherapists, pharmacists and experts on pacemakers. The group grew out of a cardiac rehabilitation programme run by the hospital. Their main function has always been to reduce the risk of further heart problems and to support patients and carers. They have a large organising committee consisting of chair, vice-chair, honorary secretary, honorary treasurer, welfare officer, membership secretary, programme secretary, public relations officer, fund raisers, social secretary, benefits officer with an editor and sub editor who produce a quarterly magazine for members.

Four people recently affected by head injuries went along to a local group. They were pleased to find many people at the meeting but came away disappointed. They had not felt part of the meeting – although someone had welcomed them, they did not have the opportunity to talk to other people whose families might also only recently be affected by accident or injury. The local group was so absorbed by the need to discuss fund-raising events and targets that they forgot to consider what this might feel like for new members coming for the first time.

Other ways of keeping in touch

Members often get more from their group if they also have contact between meetings. Groups achieve this in different ways – telephone trees to let people know of events coming up or to share an idea or provide support; letters between members or pen pal schemes with people in different parts of the country; newsletters.

Newsletters can be both an internal communication i.e. between members and a way of publicising what you do to others. Sometimes it is possible to include both aims especially if it is aimed at keeping members informed if they cannot readily attend group meetings. Sometimes the two aims can conflict. You can't always say what you want to members in a news-sheet or publication which goes to non-members. A newsletter can be a simple A4 sheet, photocopied and circulated to members. However, many groups are able to provide newsletters typed on word processors or produced on computer desk top publishing programmes which allow for better reproduction and graphics.

The growing use of computers, electronic mail and internet bulletin boards and web-pages offers new opportunities for communication between members and between groups.

There are a number of activities which are aimed at helping groups to work well. There are handbooks which deal with matters such as different ways for people to introduce themselves in groups (ice-breakers), how to deal with people who monopolise meetings, how to listen effectively, and fund-raising ideas, as well as giving help on organising your group. Very often, though, group members want to expand their skills through sharing ideas with others – through joint meetings with other active members of self help groups to talk over common organisational problems, or through training. Sometimes groups can see formal training as a way of professionalising their groups and diverting attention away from the value of their lay experience. More often, members of groups want to learn or develop new skills in order to gain more confidence in taking part in their group.

5 Activities: what groups can do

The activities of many or most self help groups will centre on a regular meeting. At these meetings members will share their concerns and support each other. Your group will have thought out what it wants to achieve, what it wants to do at it meetings, and how they will be conducted. This chapter looks at some of things groups can do either in their meetings or in addition. The group will decide as it goes along whether it wants to do any of them.

Not all you'd like to do will be possible. You'll need to take into account, for example:

- Your members' situations
- The size of your active membership
- The attitude of professionals and the community towards you
- What resources you have initially

Information giving

The need for information, sometimes to the point of desperation, is a very common need in people in self help groups. Groups can often be a very useful source of help. This can be provided by:

- Asking people with specialist knowledge to give a talk
- Compiling a library of relevant books and articles

- Producing literature
- Knowing other useful sources of help
- Getting literature from a national organisation

Professionals are sometimes concerned that self help groups will hand out inaccurate advice. You should take great care this doesn't happen. It is useful to spend time researching information relevant to your group and also other local helping agencies who might be able to give advice on a range of services, benefits and available support. National organisations often produce well-researched and reliable information. Many groups based on health problems make it clear that they do not provide medical advice, and instead encourage people to return to professional workers.

Social activities

Sometimes social activities are best when spontaneous, informal and outside the usual pattern of meetings, but some organised events can contribute to maintaining the momentum of a self help group.

Examples of successful group social events

A country walk

A children's party

A film show

A square dance

A meal in a restaurant

Theatre visits

A museum visit

A coffee evening

An outing to London

A canal trip

You'll know best what works for you, but keep it simple and cheap to start with, and have something that doesn't depend on large numbers. Not everyone will come.

> Some parents of children with autism and other communication difficulties found that when they took their children out socially to cafes and play areas, they were embarrassed by the looks given to them by other people – people who thought that their children were ill-mannered and unruly. Not going out at all, they felt, disadvantaged their other children too. As part of a group, they decided that social outings would be one of their main activities. Being together helped to alleviate these feelings and they were able to cope with a greater range of activities.

Be careful that social activities will add to – not detract from – your general aims and immediate objectives, and when they are planned bear in mind both the needs of the members and what people can afford.

Fund-raising

Some groups fund-raise, others don't at all. For a few it is their main aim. What are your reasons for fund-raising? How much do you want to raise in a year? Who will benefit from the money? Does your national organisation, if you have one, have rules about this? These are some of the questions you'll need to ask yourselves. Many groups find it another way of consolidating the group and having an enjoyable time.

Here's an example of a group who undertook fund-raising as a positive and enjoyable exercise, clearly related to the group's goals. Raising money proved an essential tool for the changes that have now taken place.

> A local branch of parents who had had a stillborn child decided that one of their aims was to get the local hospital to change the way parents were dealt with at this distressing time. After their fund-raising efforts they gave the hospital beautiful baby clothes and a camera (so that the child could be photographed), a book of remem-

brance, and furnished a parents' room. They used quite ordinary methods – holding jumble sales (some at the hospital) and selling Christmas cards to considerable success.

Campaigning

Members of your group will know at first hand just what it is like to live with a particular situation, and what enables you cope: you become your own experts. From this experience you may feel you want to contribute to the ideas behind the planning and provision of health and social services. Indeed, professionals working in the field may actually approach you, as one doctor did when wanting reaction to the way his clinic was run.

As an individual, one might feel discouraged or unable to complain, criticise or even praise services. However, a group can take up issues, quietly or loudly, to let professionals and policy-makers know its views.

One new group successfully campaigned on one issue, getting considerable publicity for their overall activities in the process.

> The secretary of a new branch of the Partially Sighted Society heard a journalist advise groups to find an issue which would interest the media, if they want publicity. The group was most concerned at the time at the plan to charge for phone calls to Directory Enquiries. They wrote letters, sent copies to the press and ended up on the front page of the local paper three nights running – and 14 nights running inside. The paper itself in fact took up their cause. The publicity about the group helped boost the group's confidence and brought in many new members. The plan to charge everyone for enquiries was quietly dropped.

> Several members of different groups for people withdrawing from tranquillisers were concerned about the lack of services for them where they lived. They also found it difficult to publicise their disquiet through the local headlines because of the labels attributed to them as "addicts". Together with supportive professionals working in the field, a committee was formed which organised someone

to carry out research into local services, and a conference was also organised. Over 100 people attended the day and a successful application for funding from health and social services was made to employ a development worker to work with the self help groups.

Providing services

Crack – the group for multiple sclerosis sufferers – provides an example of a successful service.

A large local branch decided that the need for exercise – a key thing for MS sufferers – could be met best by a weekly class for its members. They recruited a physiotherapist and volunteer helpers and booked a hall with suitable equipment. Members enthuse about its benefits and enjoy seeing each other outside the monthly meetings.

The success of the tranquillisers group, and the class organised by the MS group, provide examples of services self help groups can develop. They need careful planning and consideration, and may require a complete restructuring of the group.

6 Extending members' skills and knowledge

Once a group has started and decided what it wants to do, members will want to increase their skills and knowledge to make the group more effective. Belonging to the group gives them confidence to do this.

This knowledge and self-confidence comes in all kinds of ways – listening to speakers at meetings, contact with other members, shared activities, learning how other members handled particular incidents, discussing case studies. Sometimes it may come from special strategies learnt in the group – breathing or relaxation exercises for example, and sometimes just from support and encouragement from other members.

It may simply be that people gain confidence to take part in the activities of the group in unexpected ways:

> "There was this woman in our group," said Bill, "she came week after week, sat there mute as a maggot. Suddenly one day she produced three policemen who did a sponsored climb and raised £1000 for us!"

Letting people know where things are and how things are organised right from the beginning also establishes that everyone in the group is expected to help. This may not happen straight away, but the expectation is there if the seed is sown at their first meeting. To give a practical example, if you know where the kitchen is and where the drying-up cloths are kept, you're much more likely to offer to wash up the coffee mugs. It may be just on that level that people want to participate at first. But what stops people from going further, taking an active part and learning new skills?

What stops people joining in?

Lack of confidence. It's very common for people in self help groups to suffer from a lack of confidence – an illness may especially be a contributing factor.

Lack of experience. "I've never done anything like this before!"

Fear they won't be able to do the job. "I just don't know how you deal with the job of being secretary – I don't think I could ever do it." People may well be ready to help in principle, but hold back from fear of not knowing what to do, or how to do it.

Cliques. Any group of people, not just a self help group, can get too cosy. The positive, supportive side of close relationships is good. But if a clique is too firmly installed, it is difficult for new people to feel welcome, and members are even less likely to offer to help.

Over-formal structures. Structures are needed in groups, but they should be tools which make it work, not barriers to involvement. Formal organisation can stop people joining in, particularly in large groups.

Low turnover in office holders. One group for parents of children with a physical disabilities recognised this difficulty and now has a rule that no one can hold office for more than three years. It's easy for a few willing people to continue to take the lead, and for the rest of the group to let them.

Poor record keeping. One reason for people continuing in office may be that all the records are in their head, or maybe in a drawer in their sideboard. No one else then feels they have the necessary background knowledge to take over the position.

"I've taken on the job as secretary", said Tess, a note of despair creeping into her voice. "The person I've taken over from brought a carrier bag full of bits of paper round to my house, and it's still sitting in the corner. I can't bring myself to tackle it." She would, in time, as she'd been secretary to another type of group already, and the actual job didn't scare her. Another, less confident person might have suddenly found a good reason why she couldn't be secretary after all, and just handed the bag on.

A group for parents of asthmatic children were having an annual general meeting. The first secretary had done the job well, and would have liked to continue, but her child's health just did not permit her to carry the responsibility any more. Carol, a new member, had seen the well-kept minute book, the file of copy letters and the box of membership cards, and tentatively offered to take over, if she could have a bit of help.

Health problems and caring obligations. Some of the problems on which self help groups are based are immense. It's not surprising that some people simply haven't the time or energy to help anyone else, or to take on jobs in the group. This happens particularly if they can never predict when they will be available.

No time to learn. Have you ever tried letting a child cook a meal? It takes twice as long, there's an awful mess and the result may not be perfect. But the immediate feeling of satisfaction for you both is immense, and in the long term, it's a step to acquiring greater skills. It needs time and the adult must hold back – it's the same in self help groups. Allowing someone else to learn needs time and patience but it's worth it in the long run.

Cultural and class barriers. Barriers of class, gender and culture prevent some people from joining in to the full. Groups need to be alert to this.

Making it easier for people to join in ───────────

Often people learn just by doing something – and it may be less intimidating to do it in pairs. One group which gives regular talks to professional workers sends one experienced speaker and one new speaker together.

This can be used for other activities too. You may need to discuss an application for a grant, do an interview at a local radio station or organise a new set of posters. If you build a tradition into a group that a new member usually goes along with one or two long-serving members, you may be surprised how much they learn. They may be much more willing to take on the job next time round, and it's also much more fun.

> "You don't mind us both coming do you? You see, we've never done it before." A new branch for parents who had experienced a cot death was anxious to make links with health visitors. An invitation to speak to their training course was very welcome – but also intimidating. Janet and Laura prepared their talks together, shared their anxieties and found their way round the building. Their joint talk was outstandingly successful.

However, groups often want to provide a particular service or particular activity which may mean a more formal approach to acquiring skills – such as a workshop on preparing a budget for treasurers, a listening skills course for group contacts, coping with bereavement, confidence and assertiveness training, producing posters on computers or effective fund-raising strategies.

Local Councils for Voluntary Service and other development agencies provide short training for groups. University Adult Education centres and local further education colleges offer community access and accredited courses for individuals. National self help organisations can offer training to their local branches. Sometimes groups can organise their own training too. Councils for Voluntary Service often hold a list of local trainers that groups can pay to run courses. This can often be a good way of helping people to get to know each other and giving the group cohesion.

> A group for widows and widowers recognised the need for people to have personal befriending, especially soon after their bereavement. But they also felt that it was a difficult job to do well. A professional counsellor was drawn in to run a six week course for

some of the members on befriending and being a good listener. The group now offers a link with one of these members as part of its service of support. Members in turn have grown in confidence and skills, and enjoy being able to participate more fully in one of the group's activities.

A group ran a telephone link in which calls to one number were transferred to members who took turns to receive them, This challenging job fell to a few committed members, until they set up a short course. This included listening skills and other useful topics – but it also gave the opportunity for people to share their experience of doing such a taxing job, and to support each other. It made all the difference and many more members now take a turn.

Providing support and back-up through training for members can give an organisation credibility. Some groups organise their own skills training for members before they act as contacts for the group.

A national organisation which has local groups for bereaved parents who have lost a child runs a course for people wanting to be contacts for the groups. They ask that members be at least two years away from their bereavement and to attend the course before they take an active role in meeting new members. This gives members the opportunity to learn skills and coping techniques in meeting new members. It also provides a support network for contacts themselves.

Rose has just turned seventy. She joined a self help group several years ago while caring for her husband. At that time she had little experience of organising a group but was willing to join in because she felt she received so much support from other members. When her husband died, she decided to continue to support other carers and ex-carers in the group. Through her involvement with the group, she also became involved in other community activities – consultation meetings, district planning groups and networks for carers. She gives talks to health and social service professionals and recently went back to college to do a presentation skills course.

Many people in self help groups come new to the whole business of organising and have never had the chance to pick up relevant skills. It's not an easy task to start and run a self help group. If you are really serious about encouraging people to join in, you must provide opportunities for them to learn new skills and extend their abilities.

7 Publicity

There are several reasons why groups publicise themselves:

- To tell potential new members about a regular meeting and give them a contact person. New members will join because they are attracted to the group. Publicity allows people who have a particular problem to know that a group exists, and to make a decision about joining.
- To inform people about a particular meeting or event – maybe a talk or a fund-raising effort.
- To help in a campaign for change, or to fight a proposed change.
- To educate the public about a particular condition or problem.
- To gain public recognition and credibility.

These reasons are often related. You will need to think about the scale of publicity, the pace at which you want to grow and the methods you can use to make yourself visible and how to cope with any response from your efforts. If you seek publicity for one purpose (for example, a fund-raising event or public meeting), you may in fact achieve another (for example, a spurt of new members)

Most groups experience a turnover in their membership. If the group is not visible, and makes no effort to draw in new people, the numbers will fall and the group will not thrive. It may even expire before it has really started.

You may want to limit your membership or you may not feel safe about advertising your group because of the issue on which it is based. You will need to think carefully both about the methods you use to let people know about the group and the content of your advertising. You may want to produce discreet posters or leaflets which advertise a contact point for your group; you may want to display your materials in a few selected outlets. If there is a local self help support centre you could ask to use their address and telephone number as an initial contact point for the group rather than advertise home telephone numbers. It is best not to include full names and addresses on publicity. Many groups use a first name and a telephone number only with the best times of day to reach that person.

Whatever you chose to do, you will need to make it clear on the posters or leaflets who the enquirer will be contacting. Someone may have summoned up courage to make that first phone call and it can be disappointing and off-putting to find they are speaking to a third party. You have to think also about how you will manage this kind of contact arrangement – phoning people back after a third party contact can increase your telephone bills. Timing is also important – an enquirer may have expected an instant reply and may become anxious if waiting is prolonged.

The initiator of a group for divorced Asian women found that she was receiving hate mail and threats after the existence of the group was made public. Concerned about her own safety and the safety of women who might contact her, she arranged with a local self help support centre for them to act as an initial contact point and mail address. Details of meeting places were not given out over the phone but messages taken and passed immediately to the group.

A group for people with a mental health problems found they had to take the phone off the hook in the end, there were so many calls.

Be careful – you can be too successful, and attract interest out of all proportion to the scale on which you want to operate. You could also end up attracting inappropriate enquiries if you are not very clear about your group and its membership. This can be both frustrating and painful for you and the enquirer.

Think carefully about how and why you want to publicise your group.

Questions about publicity

What priority does your group want to give to publicity?

Does your publicity bring you new members?

Which method is most successful? Ask people how they heard of the group, when they first make contact.

Does it all depend on one person?

Have you got headed notepaper?

Do you collect press cuttings? Could they be used in displays?

Do you take photos of your activities? Could they be used in papers, reports or displays?

Are you using all the opportunities available?

Word of mouth

Many groups have found that this was their most successful method of recruitment, and it's very cheap. If it feels right for you, encourage members to talk about the group to families and friends. Recognise, however, that anonymity may be more important to people. They may come to meetings without ever telling people close to them that they do so, so don't put pressure on people to be ambassadors or recruiting officers.

Posters

The text of a poster needs to be simple and clear to explain what your group is about, who might want to join and how they might make further contact or learn about meetings. Illustrations and drawings with a few words can often demonstrate your purpose just as well. Not all your audience may be literate.

For some English may be a second language. You may want to consider producing posters or leaflets in other languages – provided you can follow this up within the group.

Think also about the life-span of posters. At first you may want to produce a poster to attract new members who are interested in starting a new group. An established group which has a regular meeting place and time and can offer services and information to members, whether old or new, will want a different poster. You may want to produce posters specifically for a given location, for example for display in an out-patients department; or for relevant professionals as a reminder to tell their patients or service users about your group.

You will need to think about how and where to display your posters, and if they are time limited – for example, advertising a fund-raising event – how to take them down too. Often personal contact, for example with your general practitioner, can result in a poster being displayed on a surgery notice-board. From this may come discussion about the progress and benefits of the group which may encourage the doctor to recommend it to other patients.

> One of the founder members of a group for people with a visual impairment in a small rural town produced very simple posters advertising an initial meeting in the local church hall a few weeks hence. They were hand-written in large black block capitals on fluorescent yellow card – black on yellow is a good combination for partially sighted people to see. On her usual shopping day, she went into her regular shops, the local post office and branch library and asked could she put up the posters on their notice-boards. Over thirty people attended the first meeting.

See posters as one of the ways that let people know you exist. You may not get many members directly, but posters will help to build up an awareness that your group is in operation.

Cards and leaflets

Small cards are another way to get general, long-term publicity. They can be given to professional workers to hand out to people they know. They take up less space on a notice board so may be displayed for longer periods. Equally, they may be covered over by larger, brighter posters. An advantage of small cards is that interested people can slip them into their coat pockets or bags quite easily and it is a less public act than standing in front of a poster writing down meeting details and contact numbers.

> A rural Body Positive group produced small business cards which could be left in health centres, genito-urinary clinics and other services catering for people affected by HIV and AIDS. Discreet enough to be held in the hand, the cards gave the name of the group and a contact helpline number. On the reverse a small list of useful telephone numbers of services and helplines was given.

Leaflets may be more expensive to produce than posters and cards especially if you want to use colour, glossy paper or several pages. A simple A4 folded leaflet (in half or in three), provides enough space for more details about the aims of the group, the activities, who the group is for and any membership details, even where the group meets and a map of how to get there. They can also be used more for providing information about the issue on which the group is based.

> A group for parents of children with a rare primary immune disorder produced posters and leaflets for their group. They knew that parents whose children had been given this particular diagnosis would recognise the name immediately but that in general it was quite rare. They wanted to raise awareness of the condition and, with the help of the national association and the self help centre, produced an

information leaflet describing the condition and how to find out more about it or ways in which people could join in or help.

Local radio

Local radio stations have proved invaluable to many self help groups. Its particular advantages are:

- Many potential members are likely to be people who can't get out of the house much and so may well be listening.

- It can get a lot of detailed information across in a very short time.

- Hearing ordinary people speaking can be much more meaningful and real than written information.

Many local radio stations feature community activities and events and human interest stories. In some areas, these features are put together by community based radio teams who are experienced at working with groups and with people who may be considering this form of publicity for the first time. This publicity can take various forms – a bulletin produced from a specially written news release, a recorded interview either at your group or in a local studio, a live broadcast, interview, phone-in. Until you build up confidence in public speaking, it may be less stressful to think in terms of the bulletin and recorded interview.

Often with recorded interviews, the interviewer will go through the questions you are going to be asked. Remember, you can always ask them to explain the format, and write down the questions. You can say what you feel is inappropriate to disclose. For example, if you have a secret meeting place, you would not want the location to be advertised.

A group for people who hear voices considered talking about their group on the radio as part of a series on mental health issues and to try to encourage more people to go along to their meetings. They were very wary of the technology and the equipment. A local radio team member went along to their meeting, spent time with them and showed them the equipment. He then arranged a follow up visit when the interview could be recorded.

Local papers

Written publicity has an advantage over radio – people can cut out the item, and think about it. This may result in them joining your group months after the article appears. Your story may have a longer shelf life because people use libraries to look at older or several editions of newspapers.

Often the subject or the work of your group alone, though vitally important to you, is not considered interesting enough to broadcast on its own. Journalists are often more interested in a personal story than in a group, and may be more willing to give space on this basis. This may be particularly true for groups just starting. You may want to change personal details or use first names or pseudonyms. In a feature article, several people's stories can be told, not just one. If the name of your group doesn't explain clearly what it does, then add a phrase which makes it clearer. You may need to remind them to include details of how people can be put in touch with your group.

Think about a local angle. Journalists on local papers will be looking for interesting events and people in the neighbourhood. Think about how you can make yourself interesting. Try to find a news angle to your subject: the publication of a report; something controversial that has happened; a local conference; a "national week" promoted by a national self help organisation. Most local newspapers run "What's On" columns which may be a way of advertising a public meeting or a special event.

There may be specialist columns run by particular correspondents e.g. a women's page, health page or community events section. It may be useful to contact the paper directly to find out the name of the relevant correspondent and send details direct to them.

Many parts of the country now have free weekly papers, largely consisting of advertising, but needing material on local news and initiatives. They have proved to be very helpful to self help groups.

Contact with newspapers and local radio stations is often by the production of a news release. A news release should be short (hardly ever more than a page). It should consist of the heading "Press release" or "News release"; the name of your group; a headline summarising the main message; the text, double spaced; and a contact name and telephone number. Ask for help from a Council for Voluntary Service or a self help support worker.

Displays

Both new and established groups can usefully consider a display. This may be a one-off geared to a specific event. It may be a permanent display which can be taken to a variety of events or used in public display areas such as a local library or shop window.

You can probably borrow display boards but if you want to make this a regular activity, it may well be worth investing in some for your group. They come in all shapes and sizes and weights so take care in deciding the one for you – think about storage space as well as delivering, carrying and setting up. Think about who can do this and whether you have members willing to staff stalls.

Make your display simple, easy to read, colourful and eye-catching. It can be an opportunity to use big photographs of current or recent activities. Newspaper articles relating to your group can be enlarged and used to good effect. As with posters, don't expect a sudden upsurge in your membership. Regard it as part of your public relations work, making people aware that your group and your problem exist.

> A local self help group with links to a hospital burns unit has a permanent display on safety features in the home. It is aimed at the general public to help avoid accidents at home, particularly those involving children.

Public meetings

Public meetings where a guest speaker or panel of speakers is asked to address the group about a topical issue can be a good way of introducing new people to the group. The event can be organised with invited guests. These might be health and social service professionals if it is about a particular issue relating to your relationship with them, or it may be an open meeting which can be advertised through the local media. It needs to be carefully planned.

Planning a public meeting

Will the invited speaker be local, or maybe from a national organisation?

Who will brief the speaker?

For how long will they speak? On what topic?

What equipment might be needed? Is there a loudspeaker system – and maybe a loop system for people with hearing aids? Who will check it is working and who will test it beforehand?

Will the speaker need a meal or overnight accommodation – if so, where and when?

How long will the meeting last? What should be the balance between informal and formal parts? How can the time be used most fruitfully?

Would you prefer a video film? Who will provide and test the equipment?

Who is going to welcome people at the door?

Who is going to chair the meeting? What will they be responsible for – don't be afraid to work it out together, especially if you haven't done it before.

Arrangements for tea and coffee.

Cost: can you cover everything out of group funds? Are you going to ask for donations? Who, if so, will look after the money?

Are you going to wear labels to identify group members?

Who is going to arrange the chairs and put them back as you found them? How do you want them arranged?

Planning a public meeting (cont)

Is there access, parking and toilets for people with disabilities? Can you mention that on your publicity material?

How much time do you need before the meeting to allow publicity to reach people?

Will you produce a news-release before and/or after the event?

Is there a photo-opportunity?

Fund-raising events

Publicity resulting from fund-raising events may be as useful as the actual cash they produce. Photographs and reports will also boost members' morale and make the hard work even more worthwhile.

Sometimes groups deliberately plan an event for maximum publicity rather than large financial benefit. Even modest efforts like jumble sales help people know you are around.

Taking part in someone else's fund-raising effort may be a particularly helpful way of combining the two aims. As well as cakes and plants, bric-a-brac or tombola on your stall for example, you can have some leaflets. Some groups get plastic carrier bags printed, or sell and wear T-shirts with the group's name or logo on them.

Television

Television is not a medium suitable for all groups. It's difficult to get access to, and the few minutes likely to be available may well be too short to put over a fairly complex picture of a group or an issue. If you live in an area where television has a particular local flavour, then it may be a more real possibility. But there are limitations and risks. Work out whether it feels right for your group and perhaps discuss the idea with one of the organisations which help to publicise groups on TV.

Groups have successfully used television in the following ways:

- Public Service announcements
- Community Service announcements
- an in-depth programme about their work
- focusing on an issue in a news or chat programme
- being part of a series on self help groups

Using other people's publicity

Can you think of any ways in which you can use other people's publicity? Are there any newsletters or magazines in your area that would welcome articles? Church magazines are one idea but there may be other publications in which you can get a free or cheap slot. The principle to follow is that of taking up opportunities to get to a wider audience, without it involving you in a great deal of time and money.

Some organisations may not be able to include your group in their publication, but won't mind putting your leaflet in their envelopes – when they send newsletters to their members or subscribers, for example. Health Authorities regularly mail to general practitioners. Using other people's mailings can be a very helpful way of getting your leaflets or cards out although you'll need to consider the cost of producing enough for the circulation and the possible charge for distribution.

Directories

Local directories are a good way of publicising self help groups. One group found they got more members through an entry in a directory than in any other way. But be cautious: a directory may take several months to compile. Will your information still be correct when it is actually published? And even if they are updated, old directories can circulate for years. People may be very willing for their names to go in at the time, but make sure they realise the implications. They may go on getting phone calls for several years.

> A small group of women suffering from postnatal depression were introduced to each other following a radio programme on the subject. They decided to form a group, and began to meet weekly in MIND's premises. As part of their publicity efforts, they took up an offer of a space in a directory of self help groups. Within months they had decided to stop meeting – many of them felt better, others felt well enough to join a neighbourhood mother and toddlers group. This was great, but health visitors, seeing the group listed in the directory and welcoming its establishment, had begun to tell people about it. Several potential members turned up on the meeting night only to be disappointed. The compilers of the directory are now offering space only to established groups.

Only consider having an entry in a directory once the group has been going some time. You should have:

- A regular meeting place
- A regular meeting
- At least two people who are reliable contacts

Don't put a phone number in if you can't deal with enquiries and if you do, then indicate if it is for general calls, or only for information about meetings. Give times to ring if that's possible.

Established groups, who can give a permanent group telephone number, could consider an entry in the telephone directory and the community pages of business directories.

Videos and computer networks

Some groups have video recordings about their groups. Often these are a result of a TV feature or working with a national organisation and are almost always professionally produced. Even though many groups have access to video cameras and use them to record fund-raising events or activities for the groups archive, making an information or advertising video for public release is an altogether different activity. There are many issues to consider in producing a video tape including issues of confidentiality, context and content as well as the cost involved. There are media centres in some parts of the country who work with community and voluntary groups and it is best to seek their advice before attempting anything on this scale.

Similarly, with the growing use of home computers and access to the internet, your group may consider advertising through various web-sites or bulletin boards. Again, careful thought needs to be given to this mode of publicity.

8 Money

Your group will need money. But think of people and their needs first, rather than money first. Don't let money, either the lack or the pursuit of it, interfere with what you want your group to do. Rather let it be one of the resources that makes it work. Think particularly of how getting money together fits in with principles of self help and sharing. Make it a positive, bonding experience rather than a drudge.

Groups vary enormously over their attitude to money. Consider these two examples.

Fund-raising: a distraction

Alcoholics Anonymous actually turns down offers of money from outside, limits the amount that any one member may contribute and declines help like free meeting rooms. In its twelve traditions, it includes the principles that:

> "An A.A. group ought never to endorse, finance or lend the A.A. name to any related facility or outside enterprise, lest problems of money, property and prestige divert us from our primary purpose. Every A.A. group ought to be fully self-supporting, declining outside contributions."

Fund-raising: a positive bond

A village-based group of asthma sufferers, and parents of children with asthma, illustrates the way in which fund-raising provided the core to group activity. The reason for their formation was to raise money to buy nebulizers for general practitioners to carry in their cars. Use of this equipment, if quickly available, could prevent children's admission to hospital. The group found great satisfaction from doing something so constructive. Through their fund-raising efforts they got to know each other better and talked about their problems.

If you are sure that money will be low on your list of priorities, then a quick read through this section may be sufficient. If your group is very interested in money – and what can be done with it – then regard this section only as a signpost, not an exhaustive guide.

Why do you need money?

The day to day expenses of running a group.

First, think about it from your situation as a new group. What might you need money for when you begin?

Costs for a new group

Rent of a meeting room

Photocopying and printing (notices of meetings, headed notepaper, publicity material, members' newsletters)

Newspaper advertisements about meetings

Secretary's expenses (phone calls etc.)

Postage

Refreshments at meetings

Speakers' expenses

Some groups, especially those that decide to limit their numbers and to concentrate on mutual support, may never need to move beyond the same kind of simple running costs as a new group. Other groups however, will grow in numbers. Once they are established, they will need money for other things.

> # Why an established group might want to raise funds
>
> Paying transport costs: For members coming to meetings or visiting housebound fellow members
>
> Taking in part in activities outside the group: affiliation to a national organisation; or conference fees
>
> Research: money for research into the problem which brings your members into the group. Some groups might even have started for that purpose
>
> Providing equipment or a service: equipment, like the asthma group mentioned above; outings; a library; specialist journals; a play scheme; publications
>
> Professionals ask for your help: with research, equipment etc.
>
> You belong to a national organisation which expects you to raise funds

Some reasons for fund raising need particular thought:

If you are asked by a doctor or other professional to raise funds for some special purpose, the group may be very glad to do this – or it may decide it is not its job. The person who asks may perhaps then be very upset when the group says no!

Your group may have been set up for mutual help and joined a national organisation for support. It may not wish to be pressurised into fund raising.

You may be asked to undertake fund-raising for special treatment for a member or a member's child. The money is directly for the benefit of one person. It may be for expensive private treatment in another country. It may be a forlorn hope for someone who faces death, and is likely to bring media attention, and sometimes hostility from doctors or public authorities. But it is not really compatible with the mutual help a self help group offers. If a group decides to do this, it has taken a decision to become something quite different from a self help group. It ought probably to keep the two things distinct, perhaps by setting up a separate trust for the purpose.

Each group will need to agree what it wants to do and the priorities it will set, in line with its own aims and purposes. If you want to raise funds for research or provide a service, well and good. But don't be pressurised into doing so against your will.

It is particularly important that the enthusiasm of a single member does not lead the group to commit time and energy to what can be an enormous and exhausting task. Groups have had to disband completely because of over-ambitious fund-raising plans and poor account keeping.

Doing without fundraising

Do you actually have to raise money at all? You need resources, but there are ways of getting some of them without paying. Can you achieve at least some of what you want to do if you get help in kind? That is, people don't actually give you money, but give you help or resources without any charge.

Free or cheap help:

A meeting room

Printing, or photocopying or use of a computer

Use of other people's mailings

Inclusion in a local newspaper (in a 'What's on' column, a letter or as a news item)

Donations of equipment

Equipment bought at a discount through local authorities

Raffle prizes

A speaker

A leader of a training course

Advertising by firms in publications, reducing printing costs

---

There will probably be a lot of goodwill in your community towards your group. Don't be afraid to tap it, if you feel the help is appropriate. Use your contacts, publicise your needs. It may be much better to put a modest amount of energy into this kind of activity, rather than into straight fund-raising or delving deep into your members' pockets.

Raising money

Most groups will want to acquire some actual money too. There are different ways of getting money both from within the group, and from outside it.

Money from members

From members: passing the hat round, a subscription, a joining fee, raffles (check the rules), bring and buy sales at some meetings. But be careful. If joining the group or coming to a meeting costs a lot, some people will be unable to join or will be discouraged.

Organising fundraising events

There are probably at least 100 different events and activities you could consider putting on. It needn't always be a jumble sale, though some groups swear by them. Whatever you do, think through what is involved.

Fund raising events

Will it all depend on one person, or can you involve most of the group?

Will it be fun?

Will it help you to get to know each other better?

How big an event is suitable for you?

Are you risking losing money?

How much time and planning will it take?

What image will it give your group?

Can you put on your event as part of someone else's bigger function?

Fund raising events (cont.)

How much will it depend on the weather?

Do you need insurance?

What is suitable for your members' age, interests and health?

Do you have enough able-bodied help?

And finally – is it legal?

Fund-raising and the law

If you are largely fund-raising from your members, or undertaking modest, informal fund-raising events, raising less (at the present time) than £1000 in a year, there may be no formal legal requirements to which you have to conform. Once you become more ambitious, you may need to check with the local Council for Voluntary Service, a self help support centre or the Charity Commission.

Check details with the registration officer at your council, and seek further advice, once you decide to move out of small fund-raising efforts.

Activities which require approval from the local council are:

House-to-house collections.

Street collections: the licence will specify the day on which you can collect.

Gaming, lotteries and raffles (other than small scale gaming and raffles where tickets are sold on the day and everybody can be present at the draw, e.g. at a fête.).

Public entertainments (the official term is "music and dancing", e.g. a disco).

Car boot sales.

Fund-raising events run by other people

Sometimes you can ask someone else to put on a fundraising event for you. They may even come to you and offer to run an event to benefit your funds.

> Headline, a group for people with head injuries and their families, gained a large income derived from other people's efforts. A village cricket team challenged them to a match, and with a little help from some well-known county players, Headline won, not only the match, but £800. The same village has an annual pram race, Headline's contribution: ten collectors for two hours. Profit: £935. Lastly, some friendly physiotherapists did a sponsored abseil and gave a major slice of the £2000 receipts to the group.

The scale of success may not apply to you, but consider the principle of asking people sympathetic to your needs to undertake a fund-raising event for you. Some organisations, like Lions or Round Table, will from time to time adopt a cause and do consistent fund-raising for it. They often prefer to look for their own good causes, but it may be possible to make a contact and benefit from it. If you are asking anybody to do this, the same rule applies as to asking for grants from trusts or from industry: you need to know exactly what you want the money for and how much you want.

Grants from Local Councils and Health Authorities

You may value autonomy and independence and fear that money from this source means you will lose them, but small grants are very unlikely to lead to control over your activities.

Grants from public authorities:

It often helps if you can raise some of the money in other ways.

Think through what you want it for and how much.

Find out if there is an official with particular responsibility for voluntary groups, and ask their advice.

Grants from public authorities (cont.)

Follow the procedure the council or health authority has set out for making applications.

Take time and care with your application, typing it if possible.

Except for small grants, you will need to enclose copies of your annual accounts and report with your application.

Money from trusts, the Lottery, etc.

This may not be a fruitful source for new, informal groups. One restriction is that most charitable trusts are only able to give money to registered charities. However, some self help groups may benefit by exploring this source.

Seek further advice, from the local Council for Voluntary Service, or from your local self help support workers, if you decide to go ahead with getting money from trusts. Be prepared to do a lot of paper work, and to wait a long time for decisions.

Trust and National Lottery money.

Local charitable trusts. A list of local trusts is probably available from your library. They may like to give a small grant to a local group.

Applying for a grant for a specific piece of work. It is often easier to get money for a particular project than for general activities.

Find out what the trust's rules are. Some large trusts, and funders like Children in Need, have a strict timetable and guidelines for each round of applications. The Lottery is becoming more flexible and now makes small grants.

Only apply for what the trust is willing to support. It is a waste of time applying for something the trust does not cover, or is not supporting this year.

Money from Industry

Think about whether your group can cope with a sudden influx of money. Changing your book-keeping systems to deal with a big grant, or registering as a charity, is a big change.

Consider whether this is more appropriate for your group. By far the greatest number of donations from firms are made locally. They like to have a caring image and to build good relations with the local community. They may not be so concerned about charitable status and constitutions. On the other hand, they are less likely to support innovation, or schemes that benefit less popular minority groups. They like to help what they see as good causes. If you feel you can make yourself into a good cause, have a go.

Some large companies in fact have charitable trusts, and you have to find out what their rules are the same way as with other trusts. Large companies in any case will almost always have a policy about charitable giving, often related to the public image they are trying to promote, and you have to find out what it is. Many firms, especially smaller ones, are more likely to donate their products than to give money.

You must make personal contact and be prepared to explain what you want and why. Simply writing a begging letter without preparation is a waste of time and annoys them.

Use the same sources of advice as for approaching trusts. If you have other contacts, e.g. the Chamber of Commerce or Junior Chamber of Commerce, Business in the Community, Rotary or trade unions, of course make use of them.

Looking after the money ⸻

Appointing a treasurer

You've thought why you need the money, and considered how you might get it. Just as important is to consider the way it should be looked after. It is essential that even a few pounds belonging to a group is properly accounted for. It's not only your public image that is important here but the feeling of trust and confidence that members of the group have in the way funds are managed.

Do have a treasurer. Other positions of authority can be shared, but you need one person handling and accounting for the money. If amounts are small, no great financial expertise is needed. You can always ask someone outside the group with professional knowledge for help.

The treasurer's job

What does a treasurer do?

The treasurer's job:

Open a bank account

Collect any income and issue receipts

Keep simple accounts of all income and expenditure

Pay bills

Report to the group on its financial state

Advise the group on what money it needs and how much it needs to raise (the budget).

Prepare and present a balance sheet and report for the Annual General Meeting

---

Here are a few dos and don'ts.

DO	**DON'T**
Give receipts and keep a duplicate for all money received	Pay people out of cash you have just received
Enter into books an account of all money received	Let money owed to the group remain unpaid
Obtain receipts for all money paid out	Ask another signatory to pre-sign blank cheques for you
Bank all money received	Let money pile up in a current account where it isn't earning interest

It's a job that needs care and conscientiousness rather than expertise with figures, and there are lots of ways you can get help if you've never done it before.

Keeping the group in touch

The whole group should be responsible for money matters – and if it is a large group with a committee, the committee has a special responsibility.

The treasurer therefore must give reports that show the state of affairs clearly: how much money the group has received, how much it has spent, what it has spent it on, how much it has left, and how much it needs in the immediate future. A word of mouth report that says there is £1000 in the bank is not much use if the group is not told it still owes £1500 for transport, rent and the costs of the last garden party.

Written reports are best and it is easy to get all the group needs to know month by month or quarter by quarter on one side of paper.

Independent examinations and auditing of accounts.

All groups should have their accounts examined every year by someone independent of the treasurer or the committee.

An independent examination can be carried out by any one competent to do the job – someone with banking, book-keeping or business experience, for example. This person will tell the group that all is well, if anything is wrong, or if the book-keeping methods could be improved. A professional audit can only carried out by a registered auditor (and not all accountants are registered auditors). Which you choose depends on the level of income of your group, the requirements of your funders and your legal status.

If you are not a registered charity, an independent examination or audit is not a legal requirement, it is just common sense. Your constitution may require it. The word "audit" is often used loosely for a simple independent examination. There is some disagreement about whether the word "audit" in your constitution obliges you to have a full and costly professional audit. It is better to make sure that your constitution allows you to choose between "an independent examination or audit", and not just an audit. If it says "professional audit" that is what you have to have.

If you are receiving substantial funds your funders may require a professional audit. They may also require you to become a registered charity, and this may be necessary if you are doing major fund-raising yourselves. You may also be required to register as a charity if you are providing services and have an income of more than £1000 a year.

For registered charities, if your income or expenditure is below £250,000 a year the law allows an independent examination, but it is generally recommended that a qualified accountant is used if it is more than £100,000 a year. Again, make sure your constitution allows an independent examination – the Charity Commissioners may be strict.

If you belong to a national association, their rules and the constitution they require you to adopt may very likely lay down how your accounts have to be examined. You will have to abide by this.

Very few self help groups will become limited companies. The rules for this are set down in company law and a registered auditor is required for income or expenditure of more than £90,000 in a year.

You can get more information on these matters from a Council for Voluntary Service, a community accountancy project or from the Charity Commissioners.

Insurance

A small group meeting as friends in somebody's house is not likely to need insurance. As soon as you start holding meetings which are advertised, and doing things in public, you need to think about it. There are some circumstances where insurance may be needed or is essential.

Whoever lets you a room may be covered for any harm caused to one of your group through their fault. Check if this is so, and check if their insurance covers negligence by someone renting a room. If so, you are covered.

If not, you may need insurance to cover mishaps through your fault to your members or to third parties – public liability (which should include your members). One possible and efficient way to get this is by affiliating to a national organisation or a local Council for Voluntary Service which includes insurance for affiliates in its subscription. If this is not possible, arrange it yourselves through a broker.

As mentioned above, if you have any kind of car sharing scheme, the car owner is quite likely to be covered; but you must check this.

If you run a fund raising event like a fête you may be covered by your public liability policy or you may have to arrange special insurance. Find out.

You can insure against an outdoor event like a spring fair or a barbecue being rained off. It is costly to insure against losing your profits, but you might cover yourselves against being out of pocket if you have made a large outlay and you lose your income. It is not worthwhile for a small amount.

You may want to insure members' property at meetings. This kind of insurance is quite difficult to get, even as part of a public liability insurance policy. It is better for them to claim through their own policies – if they have them.

9 Transport and getting together

If possible, choose your meeting place, time and day so that people can use public transport, or where there is a car-park. Consider carefully whether you need to do anything about providing transport. In rural areas especially, it might be a crucial strand in your arrangements. Keep it as simple as possible, if you do, and use other people's vehicles if you can – community transport schemes are particularly useful and valuable. But there is more than one approach to the issue of transport, as these examples show.

Anne has severe rheumatoid arthritis. Each month she organises transport for 120 members of a local arthritis group who could not get to the meeting without a lift. Transport for this group is essential. But they don't own a minibus, they use members' cars, and Anne does the organisation from her home, largely by phone.

Kath has agoraphobia. When she first started attending the phobics group the only way she would go was in the family car. As she got better, she tried the bus – as long as her husband drove behind so that she could get off if needed. Now she goes alone on the bus.

Tim has depression. He is finding membership of a group of people with the same problem helpful, but it's an awful effort to get out and get there. The group's policy though is to recognise that making such an effort is part of a commitment to self help and the aims of the group. Cushioning Tim with easy transport won't help in the long term, and could make the group into a "do-gooding-to" organisation rather than the self help group they want to be.

How does your group feel about it? The following list may help you decide.

Transport to meetings

Where do members live? Is transport essential?

How will your choice of place, day and time of meetings affect transport?

Are there particular days, like market days in rural areas, when public transport is more frequent?

Do members have a health problem which makes arranged transport essential?

Do members have their own transport?

Is it better just to assume people will make the effort and make their own way? And might it be better if they do?

If you don't arrange it, will they come at all?

Is cost rather than convenience a problem? Can you afford to offer transport?

If you decide to provide transport, are there outside organisations that can help?

Can members give each other lifts – or at least, a lift home, if they can get to the meeting alone?

Help from outside the group

You may decide to do nothing about transport arrangements. That will simplify life considerably. If so, take particular care when choosing the meeting place, time and day, so people can either use public transport or can park. For some people, e.g. the elderly, day time meetings are much easier.

If you decide to offer help to members, then find out whether you can get it from outside the group. One group's transport rota includes social services ambulances, volunteers' cars and a voluntary transport scheme minibus. A transport system organised by the local Lions Club in one town led to the attendance trebling at a group for people with hearing loss. Social services department ambulances and minibuses, used to take people to day centres, are made available in the evening to another group.

You could approach the following organisations:

- Social services departments (in Scotland, social work departments, in Northern Ireland, health and social services boards)

- Volunteer bureaux

- Voluntary transport and car schemes

- Rotary Clubs, Lions Clubs etc.

- A community transport scheme

The last may mean a minibus, but if you have a number of members with severe mobility problems, this may be exactly what you want.

Some members may have been introduced to the group by a social worker or health visitor. Ask if they can bring them to meetings, at least for the first few times.

Lastly, if cost rather than access to transport is the problem, can you get a grant to subsidise transport costs?

One group set up to meet the needs of people being discharged from a psychiatric hospital got a subsidy through the hospital social work department. It may be possible to get a grant for travel from the local social services department.

Using members' cars

This can be a sensible, easy way to help with transport. If you're only a small group, arrangements can be made simply and the job of making sure they work can be shared out. No one minds giving the occasional lift, but if it's a regular commitment, think about sharing the cost of petrol. Insurance arrangements now allow this, as long as the car owner doesn't actually make a profit (i.e. there are mileage allowances), but ask people to check that their policies cover the use of their car in this particular way.

Remember though that for many people, illness or the demands of relatives make attendance at meetings erratic. You will need to give thought as to whether a car-sharing arrangement is reliable enough, and what will happen if people can't come – or just don't turn up.

Giving lifts is not just a practical way of getting over transport problems. It's a way of helping new members to feel welcome in a group; a chance to make friendships; an opportunity to share in a small group. But organizing a lift rota is not for every group – feel free to leave people to make their own sharing arrangements if this seems better.

Other ideas for getting together

In some circumstances you may not need to have a meeting at all.

Teleconferencing.

A group with few members scattered widely across the country or a region may find it very difficult to get together for meetings. A teleconference – a number of people all connected to each other by telephone – is now practical. With the initial charge per line, the charge per minute, call charges at weekend rates and a reduction if you are a registered charity, an hour's conference for 10 people can cost only a few pounds per hour. This is much less than travel to a meeting if you are scattered, say, all over the north of England. It is a real alternative to meetings if members are housebound by their disability, and an attractive idea to someone who might help with funding it.

Community Network (address and telephone number in the Appendix) provides a service for groups with social welfare and charitable purposes

Some of the group could usefully practice on a small scale before doing it regularly.

The Internet

There are forums on the Internet for people with many kinds of condition and disability, often international. These can fulfil many of the functions of a self help group – exchange of knowledge and information, mutual support, ideas and help. A group may want to create its own web page. Obviously you need a computer and the necessary skills, so it is not for everyone. But others may prefer it to a group.

10 Computers and printing

Computers

Many members of self help groups will now have personal computers.

They can be used:

- For address lists and mailing (database programmes)
- For correspondence (word-processors)
- For circulars
- For newsletters and reports (word processors and desk top publishing programmes)
- For the accounts (spreadsheets)
- To prepare artwork for the printer.
- For e-mail and getting information from the Internet and the World Wide-Web
- For discussion forums – electronic self help groups.
- For sending faxes (receiving them is possible but a bit more complicated)

Many programes come in the software package supplied with any computer purchased in the last few years.

If you carry more details about members than just names and addresses for mailing you will almost certainly have to register under the Data Protection Act, and anyone on your list must be allowed access to their records.

Printing

Why might you need printed material?

These could be the reasons:

- To attract new members
- To inform the public and sympathetic professionals
- To communicate with members
- To share information
- To publicise events
- To assist a campaign

These are specific aims which printing will help achieve. For new groups, there is an even more basic reason why you may need printed material. It will help you be a group. Groups are surprised to find how designing even a letterhead makes them focus hard on who they are, and what they want to do. You need a name for a start. It is not easy, but it is rewarding and it is a tangible achievement. A number of members can be involved too. Indeed, if they are not, it won't be the group's material. It will appear to be that one person's only, which is not healthy for a self help group.

What printed material might you need?

Here's a list of items self help groups have produced. You won't need them all, of course, but it may help you decide what you need now. Come back to it again later on, when your group has been established for a while:

- Headed notepaper
- Cards
- Posters about regular meetings
- Posters giving a contact person
- Posters about special events
- Blank posters
- Badges
- Identification cards
- Copies of articles (with permission!)
- Summaries of talks
- Extracts from national newsletters
- Bookmarks
- Calendars
- Booklets about a particular condition
- Leaflets
- Members' newsletters
- Minutes of business meetings
- AGM minutes
- Annual reports
- Lists of useful names and addresses
- T-shirts
- Plastic carrier bags
- Calendar of group events
- Pens

Who needs printed material?

Most groups will benefit from having at least some printed material of their own. Some small groups and some branches of national organisations, whose parent bodies produce good literature, may not.

Can you learn from other people?

You may never have printed anything before – but lots of other small organisations have. Get people to bring examples of printed material from other organisations. Go – in pairs maybe – to places where there are a lot of posters, like the library, and study how effective and attractive different ones are. Would you go to their meeting?

Help

You may get help from a resource centre or arts centre in your area which offers particular help to voluntary groups who want to produce printed material. The Council for Voluntary Service or a self help support worker will probably be able to advise you.

What about cost?

Printing will cost money, but it need not be a huge sum. It will depend on what method you use and where you get it done. If you can learn to do it yourself, as many groups have done successfully, you will save money.

How can you produce printed material?

There are basically two methods of producing printed material:

The first is to produce it yourself on a computer using a word processor or desk top publishing package. This is fine for minutes, notices of meetings, and several copies of reports, grant applications and so on. If you are good at it, or have help from a member or friend who is, you can produce material of excellent quality. For small runs, just make copies on the computer. If you want more – say twenty to a few hundred sheets, reproduce them on a good photocopier. A high street copyshop will do them at a reasonable price, and if you take your originals to a professional printer they will just do the same anyway. If you have the right printer with your computer you can do coloured material for small posters, etc.

But be careful about quality. If you lack experience of layout and not are at ease using the computer the work won't look its best. If no one in your group has got a computer you can't do it all yourselves. But this method is so much cheaper for very small runs than going to a printer that it is worth getting help from a friend or going to a resource centre to make use of its computers. You may also be allowed to use a computer at work, or get help with layout and design from colleagues, art college students, occupational therapy departments, a Council for Voluntary Service, a school or a community centre.

The second way is to take the material to a professional printer. This is worthwhile if you want material of a high standard such as publicity material or reports for a large group, or if you want a long run of something where you have produced the copy, the "artwork", yourself.

You may be able to cut costs by drawing on outside help, getting sponsorship, applying for specific grants, getting discounts and paying promptly. Make sure the initial printing order is large enough – it costs more to go back and ask for another batch at a later date. Printers prefer not to do rush jobs, so plan in advance and work to a timetable. High street copying and printing shops can do rush jobs from your own artwork but may cost more. Libraries usually have coin operated photcopiers. You need a printer for complicated jobs like raffle tickets.

Photocopying and reproducing other people's material

If you are simply copying your own minutes, there are no problems. But it is illegal to photocopy copyright material, unless you just want copies of an article for private study. If you want to make and use copies of other people's material, ask permission. The same applies to retyping and printing other people's texts, except for short quotations for comment. If you use other people's material, credit them.

Other methods

Silkscreen printing is slow and laborious but is a very effective way of producing original posters and T-shirts. If you need a small number of large well produced posters a signwriter might be the best choice.

Newsletters

One invaluable method of keeping in touch with members is a newsletter. It can contain:

- A programme of meetings
- A summary of interesting meetings
- Reports on research and social, medical or political advances that interest the group
- Personal news about individuals – if they want! Remember privacy
- Personal articles, opinions, accounts of experience
- Contributions from people outside the group – doctors, therapists, nurses, social workers
- Material and news from a Council for Voluntary Service, a local self help support worker, the social service department, or the national organisation you belong to

Don't print attacks on people, services, public authorities, national organisations or political parties without thinking very hard about it. Most groups will want to avoid anything controversial like this. If you have to say something hard hitting which will cause controversy, get the agreement of the whole group before you even think of it.

Don't print personal opinions and disown them by saying they are not necessarily the opinion of the group. If you don't agree but want to give space to the opinion, reply courteously in an editorial article, let somebody else reply or put it in an "Opinion" section. You will be held responsible for what is in the newsletter whether it is your own view or not.

Look at other people's newsletters.

Keep material short and don't be afraid to edit it – though keep in touch with the writer if you do.

Think about layout. Well laid out pages, with columns, boxes and even sketches and graphics can be very attractive even if it is only a single sheet or a folded booklet stapled in the middle.

Several closely typed A4 sheets can look deadly.

The newsletter will need an editor or an editorial group as well as someone to type it, lay it out and produce it. The editor should regularly ask for views on the newsletter at group meetings and accept guidance on what goes in it – it is the group's newsletter, not the editor's.

11 Relationships with national organisations

Self help groups are essentially local bodies. Face to face contact or local phone calls will be the way most people take part in them. If there is a national link-up, and many groups have found this helpful, probably only a minority of members will be involved.

There are two types of national organisation that you might have contact with. The first are *general organisations*. Some are listed in the Appendix. They may well produce useful publications, provide advice, or organise conferences. On the whole – especially if you are new – they are several steps removed from your local concern, and you may never need to contact them.

The organisation that you are more likely to have a relationship with is a *national self help organisation*, which concerns itself with the same issue as your group, but on a national scale.

National self help organisations vary a great deal – in size, resources, aims and structure. They may regard themselves as having close links with professional care and may even be dominated by professional workers. Or they may be fiercely independent, sometimes highly critical of professional services, operating as a pressure group or advocating alternative care.

The following six types of relationship between national bodies and local self help groups are all possible.

No national organisation exists

You've no choice here. If you set a group up, it's simply a local group. If you need support, or signposts to information and help, you'll have to look to local organisations for back-up. There may be other local groups tackling the same problem in other parts of the country. If you want to contact them, you may be able to do so through a Council for Voluntary Service, or a self help support worker, but it may not be easy. On the other hand, you have a free hand in what you try to do and you can give all your time to developing your local work.

Starting local, affiliating nationally later

A number of self help groups have happily started as a local body. They may not have known that a national organisation existed or decided to delay a decision on whether to join till they found their feet. If you do this, you may find the national body requires you to make some changes in your group and you may need to give them some money. There are many benefits in starting this way, enabling you to take one step at a time.

You will be able to concentrate on establishing your local group rather than feeling obliged to raise funds or join in national meetings. And once you do affiliate you will be strong enough to decide yourselves how active a part you would like to play nationally and what sort of back-up you need from the national organisation.

Starting local, staying local

Others have started the same way but decided to stay as an independent local body. There are also examples of groups who affiliate for a time, and then withdraw from their parent national body. There is no compulsion to have a formal relationship – and indeed as the list of disadvantages on page 93 shows, there can be benefits in being totally local and independent. It depends a lot on what you are trying to do, and your priorities.

Perhaps the happiest compromise form of relationship is where local groups remain autonomous, but have the opportunity to use a national body. In some cases a local group can affiliate, becoming a kind of associate and receive newsletters, without voting rights. They may draw on it for information and advice, or use it as a means of linking up with other local groups. Whether this is possible varies from one national organisation to another.

National organisation initiates local group

You will be starting as a local branch of a national body, and will have to include the requirements of your parent organisation in your aims and structures. This will mean less flexibility but brings advantages. Remember though that some groups have found that relationships between national bodies and local branches are not wholly easy. It will be particularly important to make space in your local meetings for sharing personal problems – it's all too easy for discussions about branch rules and donations to head office to leave no time for mutual support. A group which finds this constraining can go independent when it becomes stronger.

Operating locally, but finding yourself national

This is can be an uninvited and sometimes difficult situation. You may be a pioneer in your field. Though your aims are to set up a local group, and the local group begins and operates well, you find yourself being regarded as a national resource. You will need to think very carefully about whether you want to take on this role.

This happens with groups for conditions where no self help groups yet exists, and particularly for groups for people with rare conditions, where there may only be a few hundred people with the same condition across the country. Ten or a dozen people, perhaps over quite a wide area, get into contact and start a group. Other people hear about them and ask for help. The enquiries keep coming: "Can you help us get going? Will you visit us? Can we visit you? How do we become a registered charity?" There have been examples of people being overwhelmed with requests like this. If it happens to you, you'll need to work out strategies for dealing with them. If you want to do more, the situation can develop in various ways:

You may establish a national network, not with branches but with members only meeting nationally from time to time and keeping in touch by newsletter, telephone – or e-mail forums. This is a big task and will change the nature of your local group.

You may want to refer them to a local self help support worker who will assist them to start their own group. (See Appendix for a directory). They may be in real distress. As with new members in your own locality, don't hesitate to remind them of other sources of help. You may feel you are rejecting people. Don't think of it as rejection, think of it as setting boundaries to what you and your group feel able to do well and happily.

Or you may decide you cannot keep this up. You have a perfect right to do this. Make your own local group and your personal needs take first place. If someone else wants to act as national resource, let them. You may be able to join a national association which caters for groups relating to a number of related conditions or situations.

A mother of a child with a rare syndrome advertised for others to form a local support group. When she received enquiries from different parts of the country, it became obvious that there was never going to be enough people in one area to set up a strong local base. Their group would have to be national. They sought help from a local self help support centre and registered as a charity.

Setting up a national organisation

You may consider setting up a national organisation, not because the condition is so rare and there are few members, but because groups have come into being, perhaps relating to a new issue, and want to associate. It may have branches, perhaps on a county or regional basis rather than local. This will have consequences for your local group. If your group takes this on the members who do it may find it hard to be very active in their own group, and somebody else may have to take the lead in your own branch. More difficult may be personal requests for help from people in trouble who live many miles away, and have contacted you because your group shares their condition. Be supportive but realistic about your limits.

The media

If you find yourself catapulted into the situation of starting a new national organisation be wary of the media. There have been bad examples of people's personal stories being overdramatised and overpublicised, bringing distress rather than progress. The press can be enormously helpful in the development of national organisations and issues – but be careful.

Affiliation to a national organisation or not? ——

Affiliation to a national body and independence both bring advantages and disadvantages. Whichever you opt for, the list on the opposite page may help your choice.

Relationships can vary ———————————

There are national organisations which welcome and give active support to self help groups which are affiliated to them. They supply information, help with difficulties and see mutual support groups as fulfilling their own objectives. Relationships work well, there is frequent friendly contact between local branches and the national body, and groups appreciate the link.

Sometimes relationships between local branches and national self help organisations are not so easy. There may be a conflict of purpose. For example, local groups may be concerned with mutual support and information – that is, they are self help groups – while national bodies may focus on fund-raising, research and co-operative relationships with professionals. Not all national bodies offer help and support to local groups in the way some do.

Possible advantages

An umbrella to shelter under

Practical back-up: speakers, literature, publicity material

Personal support from people with knowledge of your problem

Links with other similar local groups

Easy registration as a charity (or use of charitable status of national organisation)

Opportunities to campaign on national issues

Help with setting up projects

Rescue at times of crisis

Training and handbooks

Welfare services for members

Credibility

Opportunities to contribute to research

International links

Links with other voluntary and statutory bodies

Possible disadvantages

Wish for control over local groups

Tension over fund-raising by local branches for national body

Inflexibility and insistence on a particular structure

Conflict over aims and priorities

Expectations of support unfulfilled

High cost of attending national meetings and conferences

Expectation of attendance at national meetings conflicts with local needs

South of England base of most national self help organisations

Tension over campaigning

Too close an association between national body, professionals and government

National organisation stagnant while local group progressive (or vice versa)

Insistence on membership subscriptions going wholly or in part to national body

There may be disagreement if the local branch wants to raise funds for a local purpose or activity and the national body wants support for its central fund raising. The national bodies may set unrealistic targets for group activities and fund-raising. There will be rules about the use of the national charity number for local fund raising which may sometimes cause difficulties.

Control is another difficult issue. To what extent, should and can national bodies control local self help groups – their publicity, campaigning or relationships with professionals? National guidance can be very helpful, or very frustrating.

On the more positive side, local groups can make an immense contribution to national organisations. It is easy for national bodies of any sort to get stagnant. Involvement by local group members, as committee members or regional representatives, can prevent this happening. They are in an ideal situation to put forward new ideas and to act as a link with the membership. If groups remain parochial, national bodies will not receive the stimulus that will come from their involvement.

On a personal level too this can be productive. People who move on from purely local self help work to participate on national committees can find it exciting and fulfilling. They need to remake their relationships at local level, otherwise there can be a conflict of interest.

Fundamentally remember that your group is local, meeting local people's needs in a particular area. When you are starting, especially, this will need to be your priority.

12 Relationships with local professional workers

Relationships between self help groups and professionals can be close or loose. Each group will want to work out what is best for them, depending on how separate or near they want to be. Some groups may not want any links at all.

Many self help groups, however, have found that good working links would benefit their groups. They found many professionals who were willing to work with them.

"We couldn't wish for a better relationship really."

"We are fortunate to have a good local GP who supports us."

They felt that professionals were gradually becoming more aware that working with self help groups can benefit their work and help their patients and clients and people who use their services. Developing good links can take a long time. Groups do not always find it easy. There can be difficulties, rebuffs and investment of time and money for no apparent results.

"It's a lot of effort at first."

"He refused to put up our poster. He said we would learn bad habits from each other."

"They're aware of us – but they don't liaise."

There are sometimes genuine difficulties in the way of establishing a good relationship with professionals. They may have heard of self help groups, but know very little about them. They may see them as a challenge to their own professional status. They may be afraid that groups will hand out medical advice. They may not trust patients to take responsibility. They may confuse them with fundraising groups or voluntary service-giving organisations like the Red Cross or Samaritans.

On your own side, you and the members of your group may be suspicious of professionals because you have had bad experiences of them. You may simply want a different sort of help and support from what they offer.

On the whole, however, groups which have achieved good contacts valued them and found them useful.

"When its good, it's very, very good".

Why work with professionals?

It may help first to think through the reasons why your group might want relationships with professionals.

To get started

Professionals can be crucial in giving support, providing practical help and bringing people together when a group is getting going. Later they may draw back or be involved in a different way. Getting help when you start doesn't mean you necessarily have to go on relying on their help.

"The OT and the Physio asked who would be interested, gave us their names and provided a room."

"She gives us lots of advice though she doesn't come to our meetings."

To get practical help and support

It can be a difficult and time-consuming job to start and run a self help group. Professionals may be one source of practical resources and general support.

"We get a safe storage space for our library"

"We have a good room, free, for our meetings."

To make sure your group has enough members

Many groups have a changing membership. People may leave when their situation changes or they may feel able to cope without the group. Groups like this may need a constant new supply of new members for the group to flourish – and sometimes to survive.

To give people choice

Most self helpers feel that all people who might like to join a group should know it exists. People should have enough information about a group so they choose whether to join or not. A professional may be the ideal person to tell people about your group.

"The Sister will phone up and say – I've got a couple here, one of them with Alzheimer's – what support can you give them?"

They can only do this if they know you exist. It is your business to make sure key professionals know you exist and what you do.

"If you're going to have to spend three days searching for a group, you won't do it."

To gain credibility

Some groups feel they have to be credible in professionals' eyes to succeed. Gaining credibility may be the first step towards getting help and new members.

"Without professional back up, you're on an uphill struggle, aren't you?"

But other groups, while appreciating that being credible can be helpful, don't feel they have to rely on it. It may not be essential.

To feel valued

Good working links can demonstrate that your work and skills
are valued. Being valued is important and keeps you going when
there are difficulties.

> "You don't want medals, but you do want to feel valued."

To influence how services are provided

You may feel you could educate professionals about your problem or situation. Increasingly professionals welcome the chance
to learn from members of self help groups and so improve the
way they help their patients and clients.

You may want to campaign for change, to achieve better services for all people in your situation. Professionals may help you
find your way through the system and find opportunities.

Which professionals? ─────────────────────

Which professionals might be most helpful to your group? Target
those most likely to respond, rather than sprinkling leaflets like
confetti. Not all professionals will be interested in helping. Match
your methods to different professionals. People concerned with
the specific issue on which your group is based will need a different approach from, for example, a general practitioner.

Professionals with a specialism

You will know which professionals are likely to be most involved
in treatment or help for people in your specific situation.

Professionals giving general help

Other professionals are likely to be "generalists" rather than "specialists" – in touch with a wide range of people and problems.
They may need to know about a lot of different groups, but are
less likely to become involved with individual groups.

Specialists:

Social workers

Consultants & their staff

Nurses & midwives

Specialist health visitors

Occupational therapists

Physiotherapists

Solicitors

Funeral directors

Probation officers

Specialist teams e.g. for mental health

Sources of general help:

General practitioners

Practice managers

Practice nurses

Health visitors

Librarians

Staff in hospital Accident & Emergency departments

Counsellors

Complementary therapists, e.g. osteopaths

Specially interested individuals

It may be a better use of your time to find and concentrate on them. Not all professionals will have the same values or attitudes. You may know open-minded, progressive professionals, who treat their individual patients and clients with respect and care about what they have to say. They are more likely to support groups'

activities. Some may even be members of self help groups themselves. And supportive individuals are likely to understand the
difference between their work and yours.

> "He listens. He's interested and dedicated and understands the
> illness."

> "She knew she couldn't do what the parents are doing."

People who provide a bridge

Sometimes getting to a professional directly proves difficult. Contact with other people willing to provide a bridge can get over the
problem. Receptionists, secretaries, nurses, health visitors and
practice managers can provide a bridge to other professionals.
Ask them – they may well being willing to help.

Actions you could take

Work through the lists on the previous page.

Pool your knowledge – make a list of personal contacts
your group members have.

Decide your priorities on which professionals to contact.

Ask helpful professionals to suggest others or to
introduce you to them.

Discuss which methods are right for different
professionals.

How might you develop links? _____

Here are some general principles.

Present a clear image

Be clear to yourselves and to people outside the group what the
aims of your group are, who can join, what you offer and what
you expect.

Set out your strengths and limits

Misunderstandings can be avoided if you show you know your strengths and are clear on your limits. When you tell people about your group, you can say how it how it differs from professional services. Say what you don't do as well – say you don't give medical advice for example, if this is relevant.

Be clear on the roles professionals can play in your group.

Be open with professionals on what part you feel they could play in your group. If you feel you want to do it all yourselves, that you don't want them involved, say so. Actual involvement in the group is not always necessary to achieve good working relationships.

Try to see their point of view

It may help to put yourselves in their shoes. Professionals work to professional guidelines, their particular rules about confidentiality, or legal requirements, for example. They work in formal structures. They have family and personal commitments as well as day time jobs.

Look effective

Aim to look convincing and dependable. Many of the suggestions elsewhere in this book will help your credibility – for example, well produced leaflets and posters, or literature from your national organisation if you belong to one.

Be welcoming

The difference between an open and a closed group is discussed in chapter 3. If you are an open group, it is important to be open and welcoming to everyone who comes to join. Professionals will want reassurance that people they put in touch with you, from whatever part of the community, will feel welcome. They are not likely to tell their patients and clients about cliquey groups. They are more likely to do so if people report back to them how friendly the group was. And make it easy to contact your group.

"He was so apprehensive about going to the group – so I tried to make contact for him beforehand. It wasn't easy".

Have a principle of confidentiality

Confidentiality is important to professionals. If they feel their clients are going to be gossiped about they may well not support you.

Make the first move

You may have to take the first step. It needs confidence and the willingness to risk a refusal, but unless you start it off, relationships may never develop.

Don't do it all yourselves

Use shortcuts and other organisations. It can be a big job for a small group alone, particularly if your members have problems in their lives which leave them short of energy and time. Don't hold back on asking if there are systems you can use – mailing systems, forums, meetings or newsletters for example. Using these can save money and time and using a professional system can improve your credibility.

Keeping professionals in touch ─────────────

Here are some practical suggestions for making sure professionals know who you are and what you are doing.

 – Publicity. Use your publicity to tell professionals what they need to know about your group and to enlist their help in telling other people about it. Set out your aims and activities on a card or in a leaflet and have a simple poster. Include information on how the group can be contacted and where and, if possible, when it meets.

 – Where you can, use other people's systems of communication – Health Authority, NHS Trust circulation systems, or hospital newsletters, community newsletters or staff notice boards.

- Develop systems for putting people in touch. Think about developing systems with professional agencies so that people are automatically put in touch with your group. This avoids depending on sympathetic individuals who may move on.

- Be clear what you are talking about when discussing introducing a system. Explain you are not asking for a referral or a recommendation. You should not expect professional workers to refer people to you as they would to a consultant or for physiotherapy or dietary advice. Rather, you want all people to have the chance to join. They need access to information so they can make their own decision. They must be motivated themselves.

- Check up on whether the system is working – ask new members and professionals. You may need to change the system.

- Pass on accurate information.

- Update it when information changes.

- Keep supplies of leaflets and cards.

- Find the best time to give information e.g. on diagnosis or later.

- Use any special opportunities for group members to meet clients informally.

- Provide ways of contacting the group e.g. via an answering machine.

- Follow any agency rules.

Offer to give talks and ask professionals to talk to you

Professionals often welcome the chance to hear from group members about their experiences and how the group works. It helps them when putting people in touch. Consider whether you can do this.

Or could professionals give talks to you? Some groups invite professional speakers to their meetings. Most find that people are willing to come. Panels of several speakers often work well – there can be more of a question-and-answer session than an expert lecture. It may be useful to get several groups to combine for such a talk. Inviting professionals may lead to them understanding what you do better and to offering other forms of help.

> "He came and spoke at one of the meetings last year. Since then he has seemed to help us as much as he can."

But some groups feel that bringing in professionals as experts reduces the opportunity to share information and support with each other. You don't have to invite outside speakers.

Contact through talks, if it is appropriate, is a simple way for self help groups and professionals to interact. Interaction is very important if you want to develop good links.

Tell professionals how you have got on

Any member can be an ambassador. They can tell professionals what the group means to them. Ask new members to let their doctor or social worker know how they have got on in the group.

This can be very powerful and effective. It needs little investment of time or money.

Have open meetings

Some groups find it works for them to invite and welcome professionals to regular meetings. Others feel this intrudes on the group. One way round is to arrange and publicise occasional open meetings or even open days – again, possibly in conjunction with other groups. Don't expect big numbers, but these events give a chance to meet face to face.

Give them a chance to be involved in the group

Groups closely linked to professional care can find actual involvement works. Examples are as members of a committee, as a figurehead president, or producing a publication together. These can lead to greater credibility, access to resources and information and informal support to group leaders.

There are disadvantages too. The special nature of a group of people in the same boat can be lost. The professional may divert the group to meeting their own aims. Some group members may feel inhibited about taking part when professionals are heavily involved.

> "I couldn't open my mouth. He scared me to death."

> "It was inhibiting when professionals attended. So we moved from the hospital to a pub."

This approach needs careful thought. But if the right individual is involved, and the group feels comfortable, it can work.

Make specific requests

Professionals cannot be expected to know what you need by instinct. Think about asking clearly for specific, identifiable forms of help. This will not only help your group, it will again bring more personal contact.

Ask professionals what they want from you

Contact professionals you already know for their opinions on what they feel is needed to build good links. It's easy to make assumptions that everything is working well. You may be unaware of difficulties and gaps.

Professionals may be reluctant to suggest changes. They may not want to appear critical of how a group runs. But if asked for their opinion, it is easier to make suggestions.

A questionnaire can sometimes help. Similar groups in one area joined together to write and send out a simple questionnaire, asking what professionals felt they wanted if links were to be improved. They got 50 invitations to give talks.

Professionals may want help with research, feedback on services, suggesting new services or co-writing a booklet on how to cope with a specific condition or illness. It may not be appropriate for your group to do any of these things – but it may be a great opportunity for cooperation.

Reviewing and changing

People come and go, both in groups and in professional agencies. Situations and needs of groups change. It is best to review and to be prepared to change your links. Don't set them up and assume they are fixed for ever. Don't be afraid to assess your links yourselves and to take the initiative in suggesting changes. You may want to do this alone in your group, or jointly with professionals who support it.

When groups are changing from being new to becoming established it is particularly important to assess and probably change your contacts.

There are an increasing number of opportunities that give groups the chance to review and change their links:

- The appointment of a new member of staff.
- Government policies e.g. the Patient's Charter.
- A special event at a hospital.
- A national "Week" on the issue on which your group is based
- An annual meeting.
- Policies adopted by NHS Trusts, hospitals and community services.

Your group may very well benefit from evolving good relationships with professional workers. They won't all find it easy, but will probably be positive and supportive. They may give you a lot of practical help, and you can help them.

Self help support workers

In many places there are now professionals or small teams whose job is to give help and encouragement to self help groups. They can be based in independent self help teams, or in a Council for Voluntary service, a Voluntary Action organisation, the Community Council in a rural area, or within a hospital or Health Trust.

Some work full time with self help groups, while for some it is only part of their job. Sometimes they work together with members of self help groups, who, as volunteers, bring the experience of being in their own group to help other groups to start or change. They can advise you on the early stages, provide resources like photocopying, help with publicity and bring you into contact with other groups.

They can also put new members in touch with you. In the USA, where there are numerous such centres, they are usually called clearing houses for this reason. They also exist in Europe and elsewhere in the world.

One very useful thing they can do is help you in your relationship with other professionals – acting as a go between, putting you in touch with helpful medical professionals, getting speakers, reassuring professionals who feel threatened by a self help group. They are also often in touch with national self help organisations and can sometimes help to smooth over problems between national and local groups.

Some groups, like Alcoholics Anonymous, some of those that work very closely with a national organisation, and some groups that grow large and start providing services, make little use of their services except for the clearing house function – putting new members in touch. Others find them very useful and could hardly have survived without them. See Appendix for a directory of local self help workers.

Of course you mustn't let the self help worker run your group, any more than any other professional.

13 Drawing on local sources of help

There are other local sources of help that you could consider. Many of them have already been mentioned – this chapter summarises them and may jog your memory. But there is a question you should ask first.

What do you want help for?

First, remember three important points:

- You and your fellow members will decide on the membership, aims and priorities of your group yourselves, and how it will be run. Some small groups, who have decided to be inward-looking rather than outward-looking, may not feel the need to develop a network of support. A small group with limited membership may only last a few years, and may not want to grow. That's fine – it may be the best way for you.

- Share the jobs out as far as possible, while being realistic about the fact that some people will join in more than others. You are a self help group, and doing things for each other rather than getting help from outside may make it easier to do your job.

- Cooperation with local professional workers can lead to mutual education and support. For some groups this is all the help you need.

Bear these in mind when looking at the question of local sources of help. You may not need very much.

Reasons for seeking help

For many groups, though, it may be profitable to look for back-up and help from outside. Groups have found that there are three particular reasons why this could be so:

The condition the group relates to may hamper its work

The problem which is common to members of a group may hamper the group as well as the individuals in it. Drawing on outside help may make your group more effective. It may release your energy and time for the things you are particularly good at. How does your problem affect the group? It could be a physical or mental illness, for example, which makes communication, travel or regular attendance difficult. Members may be caring for dependent relatives. Outside back-up and resources could help to overcome these obstacles to the group running well.

> A group for people with different kinds of physical disability advertised for volunteers to help them to run their group for the benefit of the members. A volunteer may be involved in helping a particular person participate in the group through interpreting what is being said, or to help with organisation of refreshments. In this instance, although the group needs support, its members remain in control of what happens at the group.

Getting help can bring in more help

Some groups prefer to stay small. Even then, a small group with few members and few resources may spiral downwards, maybe rather sadly. Help from outside, whether practical help in the form of rooms or publicity, or good advice, possibly from a nurse or social worker, or from a self help support worker, can help to get the group back on its feet again. If the group wants to be larger and extend its activities, it will usually seek all kinds of assistance. In both cases, even if the group has only a few active members, getting help from outside sometimes seems to enable it to generate resources, stabilise or increase membership, and spiral upwards if it wants to develop.

Self help groups flourish in an atmosphere of approval

Goodwill does not only have to come from professional workers. A feeling that the whole community welcomes and admires your efforts can really spur you on. Back-up, even in a very modest way, is a way that they can put their approval into practice. Groups based on a problem surrounded by a lot of stigma or misunderstanding, even prejudice, may find it more difficult to start and to keep going. Asking for support from the local community may well break down barriers and give you more credibility.

What sort of help might you get?

Practical help – money, rooms, secretarial services and so on

Publicity for members, campaigns, spreading information

Support for key officers in particular (some one else beside a professional worker or a self help support worker may provide this)

Specialised information to supplement your own information service

---

When can help be particularly helpful? ⎯⎯⎯⎯

There are three particular times when outside help is especially valuable – whether it comes from professional workers or local organisations.

When you are starting

If you've read this far, you'll have realised that it's not an easy job to start a self help group. Many have foundered through not seeking and accepting back-up at this stage.

At times of change

Stable groups may not need much outside help. Groups who change in size, meeting place and so forth may benefit from it. New officers of groups are likely to welcome general support, and a group which changes direction may want some outside guidance. Those which change from being totally voluntarily run to having a paid member of staff will be particularly wise to seek outside advice. This has proved to be a specially difficult, though challenging time.

At times of crisis

This is more difficult if the crisis is internal: personality conflicts, perhaps, or the intrusion of religion or politics. You may be the only people who can resolve it, painful though it may be to confront each other. But a sensitive outsider may be useful as a sounding board and source of calm, uninvolved comment. Practical crises, like losing a meeting room or transport arrangements breaking down, could well benefit from help from outside the group.

From whom might you get help? _____

As the previous chapter has shown, the best source may be local professional workers. For a number of reasons, they may not be appropriate, or you may not need the type of help they can give. In particular, if there is a self help support scheme, with workers whose job it is to help groups, this will probably be the first source of help you turn to and the quickest route to other kinds of help. A wide variety of local organisations may exist in your area.

Sympathetic individuals

Some organisations and resources may be easily available in your area, others may not. If you do find relevant local organisations, remember that the individuals within them are just as important as the aims and outlook of the agency. You'll probably get most help from sympathetic people who also:

- Have relevant knowledge and insight
- Understand how organisations start and develop
- Want to see you succeed, not take the limelight themselves

You may not of course find support in the first agency you contact. Don't be disappointed if it doesn't work out – try some more. Think through your approach before making your initial contact. It will be helpful to be clear about your needs and to take or send information about your group.

When a good relationship does evolve, remember it's not just the specific bit of help that is important. Linking up with the local community and getting its support implies recognition of your group. And it breaks down barriers of stigma and prejudice.

Contacts with other local self help groups ─────

Members of several groups can share knowledge and difficulties.

> "It makes you feel you're not alone" said Jane, after a discussion evening on the relationships groups have with professional workers. She discovered that her group was not the only one finding them difficult. Jane and her group got support and practical ideas from other self help groups.

Members of groups often seem to identify with each other because they are all experiencing deep personal problems.

> "You understand, you're in the groups." Barbara was sharing a personal problem about the death of her child. She'd met some

members of self help groups, other than her own, at a conference, and found herself able to talk freely in their company. Though their personal problems were very different, she felt that as fellow self helpers they would understand.

All groups or some groups?

If you belong to a national organisation, you may well have the opportunity to meet similar groups in other towns. This can be immensely useful, but travel, time and money all limit the frequency of meetings, and areas vary so much that groups don't always identify with each other.

People have found that there is some value stemming from contact between self help groups in the same area. But should this be with all groups or just a few?

Sometimes it's very useful for there to be contact – and maybe action – between all, or most of, the groups who work in the same area. This isn't the only approach. You may benefit from smaller networks:

- Groups who are facing a very similar problem, being the parent of child with disabilities for example, can find links with other groups valuable.

- Groups which are similar in their organisation, perhaps the anonymous groups, may feel a common identity and want to learn from each other.

- Groups who meet in the same building – a health centre maybe – could find it helpful to get together occasionally.

There is room for plenty of flexibility.

Simple ways of having contact

You need to be realistic about how much time you can spare for joint activities. The following examples are some very simple ways of having contact, which don't need much time or money and which you can arrange yourself.

Visiting each other

A few people from one group can usually easily arrange to go to another group's meeting. Some, especially those based on anonymity, may prefer this to be at a specially arranged open meeting, but others don't mind visitors sitting in on any meeting. It's best to phone first.

> Liz was seeking help with her eating problems by starting a new group but neither of the two local groups concerned with eating – Anorexic Aid and Overeaters Anonymous – focused on her needs. She used her visits to their meetings to help her find out more about how different self help groups function, and to establish links with similar groups.

Liz's visits were to other similar groups. If you actually want to see how self help groups organise themselves, how they tackle practical problems or relate to professional workers, you could actually go to any self help group. Of course you must make contact and ask to attend, even if it is a group you are likely to join.

Joint sponsorship of one-off meetings

Groups are often based on one very specific problem, but they may find there is an area of overlap between them. They also often find it difficult to invite an outstanding speaker and guarantee a reasonable audience.

> Three new groups had grown up at the same time: the Food Allergy Support Group, the Migraine Group and the Asthma Group. They found a common interest in allergies generally, joined up with the Eczema Society, located a knowledgeable, well-known speaker and set up a joint meeting. The cost of publicity and the rent of a large room in the central library was split between them. The large audience of over 100 gained knowledge and the groups enjoyed the contact and working together. All costs were met by donations at the meeting and many new members joined individual groups.

Sometimes this can come about because the groups meet in the same building.

> An imaginative general practitioner welcomed neighbourhood based self help groups using the meeting room in the health centre. The number of groups grew, with sensitive support from the health centre staff, and he suggested trying out a joint meeting. It proved useful practically – and also gave a neutral friendly place for groups to talk about their relationship with professional workers and to identify weaknesses and strengths in their own groups.

Seeking each other out at other people's meetings

When groups get established, they often find themselves involved in joint activities, relating to, but outside the self help field – a hospital open day in which groups are invited to put on a display, a specific local or national campaign about disability, or allergy, or other conditions. This type of wider contact can be very useful in itself – and also gives opportunities to meet and talk to other self help groups. You can seek them out without too many problems. Even a brief conversation can bring surprising results.

> The Partially Sighted Society and the Eczema Society both took part in a display put on by the local Council for Voluntary Service. The organisers had helped by putting their display boards close together and in the inevitable lulls during the day, members enjoyed talking. They both picked up a few hints and said how much they'd appreciated contact.

Contact and joint activity where there's outside back-up

Most group members want to put most of their time into their own group. If an outsider can do some of the organising and provide resources, groups can enjoy and benefit from a wider and more ambitious range of activities. The outsiders could be local professionals. A health visitor for example, might know of a number of small groups for parents of children, with disabilities and help them get together and arrange joint activities.

Where there is a specialist self help support scheme, a self help worker, or a Council for Voluntary Service, Volunteer Bureau or Community Health Council which is interested in and supportive to self help groups, they will often sponsor or back up joint activity. What has been done?

Joint publicity and information

Groups have found that joint publicity and information can be very valuable – it both brings new members in to particular groups and creates an awareness in the community of the existence and value of self help groups generally.

- In one city, groups joined together in a monthly self help spot on the local radio, part of another programme.

- There are many examples of directories of self help groups.

- Joint posters have been prepared.

- Groups heve given joint talks to trainee doctors and health professionals.

- Sometimes groups have shared a regular column in the local paper.

Joint meetings

"It seemed to spur us on." "It lifts me up each time I go." "I love these kind of things – we get to know each other better." Self help groups in another town had the opportunity to meet at a series of summer evening discussions. They heard speakers from outside and, even more useful, from people in other groups. People looked in depth at specific subjects in small groups. The local self help support team made the arrangements and a day centre gave free accommodation.

Joint training courses

Are there subjects that you feel you'd like to study for a short time? A short course, set up specifically for members of self help groups can be valuable.

Groups in one area found that many of them were involved in listening, sometimes on the phone, sometimes face to face. It became more than befriending, and met a need for one-to one help between group members outside the meeting – but it was a challenging and sometimes difficult technique. A local counselling service put on a five session course in listening skills. This was viable because it was attended not just by people from one group but by members of five local groups. It didn't turn them into professional counsellors but equipped them with some skills and increased their confidence.

Help to new groups

With some outside back-up, it can sometimes be possible for new groups to get help from established groups on a more systematic basis than the odd visit. One experiment in a self help support scheme showed that a few long-term members enjoyed the opportunity to guide new self helpers.

> A local trust gave £500 to meet the expenses of what came to be called a "Supporters' Club". Six experienced members of self help groups became involved, meeting monthly to back each other up and get guidance from the self help team leader. The grant met their travel expenses. They were linked, either individually or in pairs, with people starting new self help groups. Though their individual problems were very different, the supporters proved to be a great boon to those starting off.

The limits to networking

The stories above illustrate the results that can come from "networks" of self help groups. But there are limits to networking. You need to be realistic, while recognising the advantages.

People's first loyalty is to their own group.

They are likely to have limited time, energy and resources.

There's a risk of getting too formal and structured.

The rich variety of self help groups means there will be common links between them.

Networks may only work over a short period of time, perhaps focusing on a particular issue of common concern.

Any network should be based on the recognition that groups need to be independent and choose for themselves how and when, if at all, they take part.

14 Changes in groups

Quite a lot is known about what goes on in groups generally. This is called group dynamics, and there are in-depth books about it which your local library will probably have. Or you could look out for short courses in your area, and they may help you to understand better what it going in your self help group.

But this book doesn't discuss things from this angle. This chapter looks at practical ways of dealing with changes that take place within self help groups.

Gradual changes that come to a head

Most groups develop and evolve. The first group of changes has its roots in this gradual kind of process. The group grows – or fails to grow. The members' needs change – perhaps as the problem that brought the group together belongs to the past or changes in nature as they grow older. Eventually something has to be done about it. Here are some typical examples of this process.

Numbers going up and down

It is very common for groups to start with a small core of interested people planning and organising; then to experience a big upsurge of membership; followed by a dwindling away and then to settle at a modest number. So if membership has dropped after a few months, take heart.

"There were only three of us left", said David, "and we did get dispirited. But we kept on meeting at my house, took advice from a friendly community worker – and now the group is flourishing".

It's not only feeling downhearted that's the problem. If you have to find a regular sum to pay the rent for each meeting, it can be very hard to keep going when attendances are small. And if you ask a speaker, it can be very embarrassing when only five people turn up – although you probably mind more than the speaker does.

And what should you do about people who seem to have stopped coming? Do you chase them up with letters, phone calls or visits? It could feel intrusive – people stop coming for all sorts of reasons. On the other hand, they could feel very touched that the group cares about them.

Dealing with falling numbers

Get donations from people when attendance is large, in case attendance drops and you need the money.

Keep going in a modest way – perhaps moving into a smaller room in the same building.

Ask owners whether they will give you a rent-free period till you get over the hump.

Warn any speaker that numbers may be small.

Consider continuing to communicate with past members, maybe by a newsletter, at least for a time, until it seems certain they are not returning. They may otherwise assume that the group has folded up.

Concentrate on the needs of those of you who've stayed.

Work together on publicity planning in order to get more members.

You'll probably think of other ways of coping. It's quite a challenge, but don't assume that a drop in numbers means the end of the group – it's all too easy to equate large attendance with success, and that's not necessarily so in self help groups.

There is also one more drastic solution to the problem. The group may have done its job for its members, especially if it is a small closed group. It may be the right time to end it. See below, chapter 16, "Ending a group with dignity."

The group decides to split

Groups split for all sorts of reasons:

- – Personality clashes
- – To focus on specific neighbourhoods – it is big enough to have a group in more than one place, and will save on travel and make it easier for new members to join
- – To concentrate on one particular aspect of work
- – Rigidity of the original group
- – Sheer numbers

Some of these provide logical reasons for change, others are a response to tension and problems. Whatever the reasons, it won't be a simple process when a group decides to split. – and it can indeed be painful.

It may be particularly difficult when resources are involved. Do you divide the bank balance equally? Who gets the filing cabinet? There's that wonderful volunteer who provides transport – will you be fighting over her? Don't let this stop you taking the right decisions. Deal openly and deliberately with it.

Splitting the group

Share the problems openly with the group.

See the split as a challenge and an opportunity for growth.

Draw in a neutral person if that may help.

If you are in a national organisation, talk to their officers.

Give clear recommendations to the group about resources.

Learn from the experience of Alcoholics Anonymous. Over the years, they have learnt a great deal about splitting. Their literature, or a talk to a member, may be very helpful.

Too many members

Splitting is one solution to this problem. Setting a limit on numbers in your group is another. It can be absolutely right for a group to restrict membership, and indeed some groups have proved to be more effective as a result. But this can be painful too if you have to reject someone who needs the group – how do you tackle that?

There may not be an easy solution, but you can suggest that they start another group with your help.

Helping a new group to start

Encourage people to set up a sister group. It might be in another neighbourhood, or on a different night of the week in the same area.

Get several of your members to go along to the new group for a while to give them support. Avoid competition.

Tell people about local organisations or individuals who might help them start a new group.

Lastly, you could consider changes in your group that allow big numbers to be a possibility:

- Spending at least part of the meeting in small groups in separate rooms in the same building.

- Changing the organisation of your meetings.

- Meeting more frequently.

Differing lengths of membership

Self help groups vary considerably in how long people remain members. If they are based on conditions like having a child with learning difficulties, people are likely to remain members for a long time. MENCAP groups are often long-established, well-run organisations, with an experienced, stable membership. But consider a new parent, facing all the problems of a newly born baby who will have learning difficulties. What do they have in common with parents, maybe now elderly themselves, caring for a middle aged adult? Is it possible for one group to meet the needs of both sets of people?

In the same way, someone who experienced a stillbirth may go on being a member of a group years after the event. A newly bereaved parent could have very different needs.

Long term changes in the group

Recognise the change and bring it out in the open.

Maintain a sufficient mix of members.

Encourage the establishment of sub-groups to meet particular needs.

Provide a range of activities, which allows choice in the way members are involved.

Make use of a variety of methods of communication.

Consider having separate groups for different age groups.

Changes in goals and objectives

When a group starts it should set out its overall goals, specific objectives and priorities. You probably at least work to a generally agreed set of objectives. As groups grow, it's possible for there to be a shift – perhaps unconscious – in what you are trying to do. Change can be beneficial: sometimes groups can become stuck if they don't alter what they are doing.

But if the change is a bit muddled or unnoticed, it can be confusing and bring difficulties. For example, new members may come to a group after reading its literature, expecting a particular form of help and be disappointed, even distressed, when it has been superseded by other activities.

> "I went to the group for help in dealing with my skin condition,'
> said Karen, "and all they wanted to do was talk about the next
> jumble sale"

She never went back. The group's literature said they provided
support. In fact, it had turned into a fund-raising group.

This kind of change is one of the reasons why groups should
evaluate their work. It can then look to see if its aims remain the
same. If you do this you will be able to anticipate changes in the
group and deal with them when they come. In addition to the
kind of formal evaluation discussed in chapter 17, you can also
use your Annual General Meeting to undertake a simple review
of the past and discuss priorities for the future.

Remember to tell other people if you have made substantial
changes to your objectives:

- Use an Annual General Meeting to undertake a simple
  review of the past and to discuss priorities for the future.

- Rewrite your leaflets and posters if you have made
  substantial changes to your objectives.

- Issue a press release (a good excuse for some publicity)
  about the way you have changed.

This need not be a heavy enterprise – but you should be alert to the
fact that groups' work does change, and it's best to recognise this.
See it as a positive, healthy development rather than a problem.

Changes that alter the nature of the group ⸻

Sometimes a group changes in a much more drastic way, when
the group – usually one which is not only successful but has
become large – takes on some new task. If this happens to a group
that started as a small personal support group it will change it out
of all recognition.

Providing a telephone contact point

This can come about without you intending it from the simple action of providing a telephone contact point. As discussed earlier,

you need to make your group accessible, but advertising a telephone contact point is not as simple as it sounds.

You may have intended it as just a way of giving information about the group and its meetings. But people ringing up about the group will take the opportunity to talk about themselves and their problems, and ask for your advice. The American Self-Help Clearing House has several pages of good advice on this situation in its book *The Self Help Source Book.* A phone contact point is not a help line; it is not a telephone advice service. You need to have listening skills, and you need to have the necessary information to handle the enquiries. But the purpose is to inform people about your group. If the caller wants more, whoever is taking the calls needs to know what to do.

Taking calls as a telephone contact point

Use the techniques of a good telephone listener: welcome the caller; use their name if they give it; encourage them to talk if they clearly need to.

Have information about your group to hand and in your head (purpose, meeting place, times, how wide ranging the group is, subscriptions if any).

You need to be able to help with problems about coming to the group - transport, uncertainties.

You may be asked for advice about the individual's problems, or expected to listen at length to their story. Be clear about what you can and can't do. By all means listen and encourage the caller to talk. Be cautious about sharing your own experience - it may or may not be helpful.

Be ready if necessary to refer the caller to someone else - to another group, if you are the wrong one, or to a regular advice agency or a specific service, if that is what they need.

Be very careful about giving advice or information - only do it if you have the information to hand and you know exactly the implications of what you are telling the caller.

> ## Taking calls as a telephone contact point (cont)
>
> Have clear in you own mind what you are going to do if the caller is in crisis. In general calm the person down and refer them to other sources of help like Samaritans, get their consent to call for emergency help - or whatever is appropriate.

If you go on doing this for a long time, it may all become too much; you become overwhelmed, or even burnt out. Think ahead to avoid this happening.

Don't forget that a local self help support service, self help worker or clearing house may be willing to take initial enquiries and let you use their number instead of the home number of one of the group.

Help lines

You may come to feel from your experience of providing a contact point, that there is such a demand that you have to establish a regular service. Setting up a help line is a really big change for a self help group. It needs organisation, information, training, and funds. It is mentioned here only because it is possible to drift from providing a contact into running a help line, and because some groups may come to feel there is a need they should respond to.

If you decide to do this, you can get help from the Telephone Helplines Association. You are then becoming a service providing organisation.

Becoming an organisation that provides services

Some groups begin as mutual support groups, and change to being organisations that provide services. The service may take all kinds of forms: day centres or lunch clubs for members or people in their families; help lines; transport to centres or meetings. You may be providing a valuable service that no one else will do. You may be tapping unused resources. And you may be acquiring yet another set of skills and knowledge.

This will greatly change the nature of your group. It will be difficult to meet the needs of members, especially newcomers who want to share problems, at the same time as managing resources. You will probably be faced with the problem that people will use your services, but not be willing to take a share of the work.

Ways of approaching this type of change include:

- Acknowledging that you are now a different sort of group.

- Making sure there is still room for mutual support.

- Splitting the group - one organisation (or one committee) may provide the service, while the other members of the group continue as a self help group for mutual support.

Some national organisations will have some branches which provide services and others which are self help groups. But a service providing organisation and a self help group are different things.

If you take this step, there are many things that have to be considered, especially if you are providing services on a large scale: employment, contracts with local authorities and health authorities, leasing or buying premises and so forth. A starting point for a voluntary organisation doing this is the local Council for Voluntary Service and the publications of the National Council for Voluntary Organisations.

Starting or becoming a national organisation

The reasons why a self help group, providing mutual support to its members, may turn into a national organisation, were discussed above (pp 90-92). In some cases, you will still be a self help group, perhaps with members with a rare condition, scattered across the country. In other cases, you may turn into a more complex association, with branches as well as individual members, and even providing services. If your group makes this kind of change, you can seek help from a local self help support centre or a local Council for Voluntary Service. Joining the Long-term Medical Conditions Alliance (see Appendix) can bring you into touch with other small national organisations.

15   Raising awareness and campaigning for change

Do you think of yourself as a pressure group? Some self help groups, including groups based on anonymity, decide that they will not be involved in any activity that involves comment on services or in promoting change. Other groups are based on an issue which means that campaigning for resources and a change of attitude is the core of their work. In between come groups – probably a majority – who see mutual support as their main objective, but also wish to take up issues, raise awareness and campaign for change.

Members of self help groups are often well-placed to contribute to discussions on resources and policies. They are informed consumers. But how do you feel – as an individual – about feeding back your opinion, maybe a critical one, to professional workers in the health and social services? Probably uneasy. You may depend on them for care and services, and you probably appreciate what they do for you and your family. An individual will find it hard to do. A self help group can comment more easily.

Why might you choose to campaign – and for what?

You might wish to campaign or raise public awareness for a variety of reasons. Here are some questions to help you decide.

Why might you want to campaign at all?

Is there a desperate need for particular services for members of the group and their families?

Do you want to campaign on behalf of all people experiencing the problem, and to increase services and resources so everyone benefits?

Do you see a need for change in the way services are provided and organised?

Do you want a big increase in resources?

Do you see a need for more co-operation between different departments or professions?

Do you want users of services to be more involved?

Do you want to educate the public about your condition?

What will people think of your action?

With many conditions, there is likely to be a lot of public sympathy and support for groups who press for better services. Groups based on a condition that attracts less public approval, often already feeling stigmatised, may find it a harder battle to win support for their campaigns.

Professional workers are likely to be ambivalent in their attitudes. Many of them will welcome attempts to increase resources and improve services – it is what they may well be trying to do too. The group may simply be trying to raise awareness of the condition. In this case, you should be able to work in harmony, as a team. Some campaigns, however, challenge professional services. Groups running them may be seen as trouble-makers.

Professionals tend to be very possessive about their job and their skills. Your campaign may be asking them to share knowledge and prepare policies jointly, so they may feel threatened. Some could also fear they might lose their jobs if far-reaching changes were made. And it is never easy to accept criticism. There will be approval and sympathy, but there will also be opposition and tension. You are likely to be walking on a tight rope between the two.

A job for the whole group?

> A Home Births Support Group was started by a group of women who had been able to have their own children at home, and were very committed to the idea of women being able to choose where to have their baby. While recognising that some births are safer in hospital, their research showed that many are just as safe at home. Their group focuses on efforts to make home births an option and so for services to be easily available. While also giving each other support, their group is centred on a campaign.

In this case, the whole group – which has a small membership – is involved in working for change. This need not necessarily be so. Some groups find it works well for a small sub-group to be responsible for pieces of work, and people who are particularly interested in this aspect of a group's work can become involved as they wish. This avoids the problem of pressing people to be active when they just need support for their own situation.

How can you achieve change?

Campaigning may involve specific action, and it can also be interwoven among a variety of self help group activities.

Mounting an active campaign

A branch of the Schizophrenia Fellowship mounted a campaign for a day centre, even demonstrating at County Hall. A group of parents of children who sniffed glue collected 500 signatures on a petition asking for a ban on glue sales, and presented it to their MP. A branch of the Eczema Society wrote to head teachers, sending them literature about eczema, offering to come and talk and clarifying issues like children swimming.

Inviting speakers

Groups have found that inviting speakers has two-pronged success. They learn from the talk, but it also gives them an opportunity to feed back experiences and educate people in positions of authority. Groups have successfully invited consultants, councillors and members of health authorities with this aim.

Fund raising for equipment

Quite modest fund-raising efforts can provide equipment that changes the way services are provided. A stillbirth group, for example, influenced the care given to parents by the resources such as the parents' room, that it provided for the hospital. An asthma group helped prevent hospitalisation by equipping general practitioners with nebulizers. For this to be successful, there must however be cooperation and trust, and it's as well to involve the professionals concerned in planning what you do.

Taking part in formal consultative bodies

There are increasingly more opportunities for consultation and participation in decision-making through formal bodies. What these are will depend on where you live. Community Health Councils, (in Scotland, Local Health Councils; in Northern Ireland, District Committees) welcome voluntary groups as members. Joint planning and commissioning initiatives involve voluntary representatives. Some doctors' practices have Patient Participation Associations.

Recent initiatives are likely to make it easier for self help groups to influence services in this way. Research on the theme of Patients in Partnership in the National Health Service has shown the value of wide consultation with patients and patient organisations by Health Authorities when commissioning services. The more this ap-proach becomes accepted and established, the more there is likely to be consultation initiated by the Health Authority itself – and not only with branches of national self help organisations, but with local groups.

A report on a research project run by the Long-term Medical Conditions Alliance shows how this can work well.

Self help groups find taking part in any of these activities can be time-consuming and challenging, but it does give opportunities for comment and influence.

Doing some research

This may sound rather high powered! National organisations are well placed to do this in a professional way but local groups can also find out facts, draw them together and make recommendations. Some have successfully asked students on a social work course to undertake surveys and write reports. This approach gives you hard facts to back your case and deals with the possible criticism that your campaign is not based on real need, but only on the claims of a few vociferous individuals.

Seizing opportunities as they arise

Other opportunities to influence services and raise awareness arise from time to time.

- Giving a talk to professional workers about your group, and using discussion to feed back comments on *their* work.
- Commenting in the press on reports and news items.
- Responding to requests for comment from consultants on the way their departments' services are organised.
- Talking to officers and members of public authorities whenever you happen to meet them.

Campaign alone – or with other organisations?

Some issues may be so specific that you feel you must pursue them alone, and you may be in a stronger position if you do so. With other issues though, you may be more effective through forging an alliance with other local organisations. They may be other self help groups; organisations concerned with the same issue; or an umbrella body of some kind. This will help prevent isolation, share out the jobs and make it easier to meet the costs.

Sometimes an unexpected ally can appear, and even take over a campaign for you – the local paper or radio station has often proved to be a more effective campaigner than the group that started it all off. Don't despise such an offer – but be careful. The media have a different agenda from a self help group.

For groups with a national organisation, there is also the option of alerting them to a need, and asking them to take action. This could be very appropriate for a national issue but won't take care of any need for local change.

However you plan to put on pressure, you may want to draw on outside sources of help for advice. For example, you may need to know the structures of public authorities and the right timing for a campaign. It's no good trying to bring about change when an irrevocable decision has been made. Organisations like a Community Health Council or Council for Voluntary Service may be very useful.

What might the benefits be? _____

- You may achieve the changes you set out to get – and receive credit for your action.

- You may see other people do what you suggested, but have to hold back your natural protests that it was your idea. You will still have achieved your objective.

- You may get more members – campaigning usually results in useful publicity.

- It may help members feel their life has more purpose – at least they are doing something to help people coming after them.

- And, as in so many self help group activities, you will find that people will grow in confidence and skills.

Is this playing politics?

It's not party politics in the sense of Conservative, Labour, Liberal Democrat, Green, or Nationalist, but you can't escape the fact that in campaigning you are being political. You are contributing to debates on policies and to decisions on resources. You are influencing public opinion and asking for change. Not all groups will choose to work in this way, but there is no need for those who wish to do so to hold back.

16 Ending a group with dignity

Ending a group may be a surprising subject to find in a guide to starting and running them. But stopping a group can be a taboo subject which people find difficult to air. And there is a hidden assumption that if something ends, it must be a failure. It's not necessarily so. It can actually be a brave, positive step. Consider these ways which may help you end a group with dignity, and a sense of achievement.

Self help groups come and go

It's a fact of life that not all self help groups are permanent. Every year some groups in an area will come to an end. This is one of their features which makes them different from more established voluntary organisations. It is not unusual for groups to end.

Some groups are more likely to close than others – it depends to some extent on the problem on which they are based. Other groups may last a very long time. But if the common factor is a temporary change in your life, you'll probably only stay in the group for a while and the whole group is also more likely to disband. It can be better to close in a sensible, organised way if the need for a group has passed, rather than to continue beyond the end of its useful life.

Why do groups come to an end? _____

There are lots of possible reasons for ending and groups may close for one or more of them.

Why groups ended – positive reasons

Members got better. They had benefited from the group, but found they could now draw support from friends, family and community groups.

The people starting the group agreed from the beginning only to meet for a set number of meetings – 10 or 20 say – and then to disband, rather like an evening class. It's called a time limited group.

The group was set up as an experiment from the start – it was a tryout, and the people concerned decided not to continue it.

The need for a group passed. Professional treatment or research made real progress and people found they could cope.

Why groups ended – other reasons

The group met the needs of a stable number of people, but did not seriously attempt to bring in new numbers. When members left, the group just faded away.

The group depended on one or more key charismatic figures. When they left, the group fell apart dramatically.

A national organisation made the local branch close, because it wasn't fulfilling the conditions under which they asked their local branches to operate.

Personality conflicts led to people leaving and the group became unworkable.

The intrusion of strongly held religious beliefs into what appeared to be a neutral group brought too much tension.

Why groups ended – other reasons (cont)

Just too many things against it – a combination of personal illnesses or pressures; opposition from professionals; apathy; lack of a meeting place and resources; members spread out over a wide area.

The group presented an uncomfortable challenge to the community. For example women who had previously stayed at home came into public view, so leading to disagreement with their husbands; or the issue on which the group was based aroused hostility and proved unacceptable.

A group for incest survivors had been meeting regularly for quite a while and thought they had a problem with communication. After talking the situation through with a self help worker, what they discovered was that they had all formed friendships within the group, met each other for coffee and shopping between meetings and gave each other support this way. They turned up to every weekly meeting out of habit rather than need. They decided to close the group with but agreed to help anyone who wanted to set up a new one.

Is it possible to make ending a better experience?

The list above begins with a number of quite acceptable reasons for ending a group. It should not take much to come to terms with its closure if the reasons are straightforward and understandable. In fact, closing can be a very positive step, leading to other developments. But further down the list, the possible situations are less comfortable. It's almost bound to be difficult and a certain amount of feeling of failure may be inevitable. These are suggestions of ways which may help ending a group to be a better experience.

Steps to end a group

Accept that ending a group is not unusual, and don't feel a great burden of guilt about it.

Bring in a supportive outsider to help you think through your decision, if that would be helpful. Some groups need to be reassured that they are doing the right thing.

Evaluate and celebrate what you have achieved while you were in existence. What have individuals gained from the group? What have you done to educate the public about your problem? Make a short list of questions and discuss them together.

Have a final meeting. It's sometimes easier to accept the loss of something if you have a ritual to go through, an event that marks the end. Even if it's just a handful of members, it may help to meet formally for the last time. People may want to say things they'd not been able to voice before.

If you have ended your group on a positive note, or even if you haven't, consider publicising your ending. This will inform potential members that you are no longer around; you can highlight all you have achieved, and it may encourage others to start up another group.

Pass on your resources to be used in a positive way. Any money left in the bank account could help another group.

A hospital might welcome a plant or a picture – the exact use is up to you. (A registered charity has to pass on its assets to another similar charity).

Tie up loose ends as much as possible.

Ways of preventing a painful ending _____

It may be inevitable that a group ends, but there are steps you can take early on in its life which will help prevent its closure, if it occurs, being too painful. These suggestions will also be helpful if you are successful and the group flourishes.

> ### Making ending easier
>
> Be realistic about setting up a new group. It may or may not work – you will wait to see what happens.
>
> Agree to meet for a specific number of meetings, then review your future.
>
> Don't let your group be listed in a directory of any kind before you are sure of its future.
>
> Record what you do as you go along – minutes, diary, photos, scrapbook, copies of letters. You may be able to leave it with a helpful outsider in case someone in the future starts a similar group. They'll gain from your experience and you'll feel more positive about it.

End with dignity _____

Self helpers themselves should be the ones who decide to start a group – similarly you should be the ones who decide to end it. It may be a positive, sensible step. If you can evaluate what you have achieved. You may find that you've done a lot: there are bound to be some good results.

Realistically though it will not always be a pleasant experience. Perhaps it will help to know that it can be painful and distressing, and that others have gone through it.

17 Evaluating your work

Self help groups of all kinds are growing rapidly in number. But just because something exists, does it work? If the members find the group is not meeting their needs, they will stop attending. The group may meet the needs of only a few, because you never asked yourself whether what you are doing is what you set out to do. Is your group effective? Is it possible in an organisation like a mutual support group to measure effectiveness anyway? How might you do it?

Why evaluate?

- When your group started, what was the exact original problem around which it was formed? You may need to redefine it or decide whether it is still as true today as it was then.

- Your group will have goals – set out in writing or based on general agreement. If you decide to evaluate what you are doing, you can go back to your goals and see if you have fulfilled them.

- Groups change. Members come and go and their needs change. Most groups need to take change into account – do you need to change your goals?

- What resources do you have – and could you use more?. Evaluation helps you look at your resources, decide whether you are using them efficiently, and maybe whether to seek more.

- Lastly, although evaluation may challenge you and even make you feel uncomfortable, it also allows you to measure achievements.

Who benefits?

- Yourselves. Your group was set up to meet your own needs and those of people experiencing the same problem. You will want to measure your work, and the way you do it, for yourselves.

- Supporting organisations. You will find that supporting organisations will be more likely to go on backing you if they know you assess yourselves.

- The outside world. Many groups will want to put over a good image to the general public, potential members or organisations which they might be trying to influence. Evaluation helps you put over a clear, accurate picture of yourselves.

Who should do it?

You and your fellow members are best placed to look at yourselves, to do a piece of self-evaluation. You have the experience of membership and access to information and you can gear the exercise to the needs of the group. It also gets over the problem of confidentiality. Most groups, if they do any evaluation, will probably want to do it themselves.

If your group is small, involve everyone in the evaluation. If it's large, you'll need to think of another way. You should certainly ask everyone their view – a simple questionnaire may help. But a small working group may be necessary to pull it all together.

In larger group, the whole committee should not do the

evaluation. A committee alone assessing a group may simply confirm their way of doing things is right. One or two committee members and one or two people who are not on the committee would be better.

Occasionally an outsider may prove to be a useful sounding board. One group found a morning with a sympathetic community worker helped them review their original aims, what their resources were and what they wanted to achieve in the future. Rather than close the group, as they'd feared, they were able to restart, refreshed and with new priorities.

If you do invite someone to do give this sort of help, they need to know the group. They should either have some insight or particular qualities which enable them to help you look at yourselves. Be cautious in your invitation and be specific about what you want an outsider to do.

Lastly, a neighbouring branch of your national organisation, if you belong to one, might be helpful in helping you make an assessment.

What will you produce?

The evaluation should always result in a written document. It can be circulated to members, given to people who help the group, and to funders if there are any, and referred to, to see if anything has been done about it. This need not be a large document. For a small group that does its evaluation at one members' meeting, it may be no more than a page or two, or even a section in the notes of a meeting.

Some things should be found in all evaluations:

- A statement of goals and objectives – perhaps revised

- A reference to the previous evaluation if there was one

- An account of the present situation

- Identification of problems, needs for change and improvements

- An action plan with a timetable – or a request for the group to produce one in a given time

What might you look at? _____

Some of the benefits of membership of self help groups are imm-
easurable. But you can ask what your members think and feel about
them. Your members are not customers, but you can ask them the
kind of question a business would ask about its customers. Don't
forget that the members you have probably like what you offer. It
is not so easy to the ask the people who didn't, and left. Other
parts of your group's organisation can be measured – at least on a
scale of good, bad or in between – and your working group has to
ask these itself. In the box is a list of questions and concerns that
will apply to the self-evaluation of most groups. Most of these can
be put to members in some sort of questionnaire or at a special
meeting.

Questions at evaluation

Goals	Why was the group started?
	Is the reason for it existing still the same?
	Are our aims what we still want to do?
Meeting needs	What do members want from the group?
	Are they getting it?
Membership	Are we attracting all the members we could?
	Does everyone feel welcome?
	Do we exclude anyone?
	Has the group changed? How and why?
How well does the group work?	Who gives the group leadership? Does it work?
	How well do we communicate in our group?
	How readable and attractive are our publications for members?
	Does our choice of meeting room help our group to run well?
	Do we have too little money? Enough? Too much?
	Can we do anything about transport, and should we?

Links outside the group	How readable and attractive are our publications for others?
	Who reads our publicity? What effect does it have?
	What benefits do we get, or might we get, from national links?
	What professionals do we know? Does it help?
	What local organisations do we know?
	What benefits do we get?
Developments	How many members take on jobs? Can we extend our skills?
	Do we campaign, or might we? How and why?
	Do we need to offer any direct service to members?

You may need to add different questions. If your group carries out any kind of campaigning or provides a service you must obviously evaluate that as well.

Some questions need an answer in some detail; others require a simple yes/no/partly answer.

Collect information ———————————

Evaluation makes you look back – but if you've nothing to look back at it will not be an easy exercise. It's important, if you can, to build in collection of information right from the beginning. It needn't be elaborate and can be tackled in a variety of ways, planned to suit your group.

What are you going to do about it? ——————

Evaluation helps you to look forward too. The conclusion of every evaluation, and the most important part of the report that should come out of it, consists of proposals for the future. If there are problems, or deficiencies, the evaluation should either propose what should be done to remedy them or formally recommend to the group or committee that proposals should be made. A timetable should always be set for this, otherwise nothing gets done about it.

Useful information for evaluation

Keeping records of meetings. Anything from formal minutes to a short diary entry or log book.

Asking people how they heard about you. If it's done automatically but sensitively as soon as they make contact, and recorded, you will have an easy way of evaluating your publicity efforts.

Keeping a scrapbook. Photos of activities, programmes and invitations, newspaper articles or advertisements pasted into a scrapbook – let you look back and enable new members to share the past.

Keep a second copy of letters and file them in date order.

When should you do the evaluation?

A formal evaluation, with questionnaires and a working group, need only be done every two or three years. But the report goes on being used in between.

Using an evaluation

After it has been produced, you refer to it to see if its recommendations have been carried out on time.

When the annual report is being done, the evaluation report provides a framework for assessing the group's work in a less formal way.

If problems arise, the report may be useful to indicate why.

If someone proposes changes, the report can help you to see where – or whether – they fit in to what you are doing already.

If changes happen piecemeal, you have a model for dealing with them.

New groups may find an evaluation, done in this way, useful to get a clear picture of how their group is developing. They may want to ask the same kind of question, less formally, but more often.

Getting something out of it

The evaluation will be useful in ensuring the group doesn't just drift, or change its nature unconsciously, and also to identify and make necessary changes. It is also an opportunity to count your achievements. Self help groups have to overcome many hurdles, and sometimes you may feel the journey you're undertaking is just too hard. Perhaps you think you're running on the spot, rather than getting anywhere. Evaluating yourselves will bring satisfaction – you will be surprised at what you've done.

Self help groups are special. You are one of many people with a problem doing something for yourself. You are all facing not only an individual problem, but also the issues that groups have to tackle. Don't forget you have strength, knowledge and skills – you are bound to achieve something, and you may achieve a lot.

Appendix

Sources of help

Action with Communities in Rural England (ACRE)
Promotes community development in rural areas.
Comprehensive advisory and information service. Represents
views of Rural Community Councils.
Somerford Court, Somerford Road, Cirencester, Glos. GL7 1TW
Tel: 01285 653477 Fax: 01285 654537

British Association of Settlements and Social Action Centres (BASSAC)
Provides resources and help for self help community
initiatives.
1st Floor, Winchester House, 11 Cranmer Road, London SW9
6EJ Tel: 0171 735 1075 Fax: 0171 735 0840

Broadcasting Support Services (BSS)
Provides training on running helplines.
Union House, 65-69 Shepherds Bush Green, London W12 8UA
Tel: 0181 735 5000 Fax: 0181 735 5099

Charity Commission
The Charity Commissioners can provide advice and
information on becoming a charity and duties under the
Charities Act 1993. They produce a series of information

leaflets. There are three Commissioners' offices from which
information can be obtained.
St. Alban's House, 57-60 Haymarket, London SW1Y 4QX
Tel: 0171 210 4477
Second Floor, 20 King's Parade, Queen's Dock, Liverpool
L3 4DQ Tel: 0151 703 1500
Woodfield House, Tangier, Taunton, Somerset TA1 4BL
Tel: 01823 345000

Community Network
Provides telephone conferencing facilities to charities and not-
for-profit organisations. Up to ten people at a time can join in on
one telephone conversation and no special equipment is needed.
2nd Floor, 50 Studd Street, London N1 0QP
Tel: (head office) 0171 359 4594 Tel: (bookings) 0171 704 0404

Federation of Independent Advice Centres (FIAC)
Promotes the provision of independent advice services to the
public across the UK.
13 Stockwell Road, London SW9 9AU Tel: 0171 489 1800

Long-term Medical Conditions Alliance
An alliance of around 70 national voluntary organisations
concerned with long term medical conditions.
Unit 212, 16 Baldwins Gardens, London EC1N 7RJ
Tel: 0171 813 3637 Fax: 0171 813 3640

MIND: National Association for Mental Health
There are many locally based MIND organisations. Details
from national office at Granta House, 15-19 Broad Way,
London E15 7RJ Tel: 0181 519 2122 Fax: 0181 522 1725

National Association for Patient Participation
Promotes the views of patient groups in primary care (general
practice).
Vine Cottage, 60 Park Street, Kingscliffe, Peterborough
PE8 6XN Tel: 01780 470437 Fax: 01780 470557

National Association of Citizens Advice Bureaux (NACAB)
Over 700 CABx and many other advice services use its information system.
115-123 Pentonville Road, London N1 9LZ
Tel: 0171 833 2181 Fax: 0171 833 4371

National Association of Councils for Voluntary Service (NACVS)
There are over 230 CVS throughout England.
3rd Floor, Arundel Court, 177 Arundel Street, Sheffield S1 2NU
Tel: 0114 278 6636 Fax: 0114 278 7004

National Council for Voluntary Organisations (NCVO)
Provides information, training, legal, advisory and membership services for national and local voluntary organisations.
Regent's Wharf, 8 All Saints Street, London N1 9RL
Tel: 0171 713 6161 Fax: 0171 713 6300

National Information Forum
Promotes better provision of information for people with disabilities.
Post Point 228, Proctor House, 100-110 High Holborn, London WC1V 6LD Tel: 0171 404 3846 Fax: 0171 404 3849
Due to move early 1998, but telephone no. will remain the same.

Northern Ireland Council for Voluntary Action
Co-ordinates and develops voluntary action in Northern Ireland
127 Ormeau Road, Belfast BT7 1SH
Tel: 01232 321224 Fax: 01232 438350

Scottish Council for Voluntary Organisations
Co-ordinates and develops voluntary action in Scotland.
18/19 Claremont Crescent, Edinburgh EH7 4QD
Tel: 0131 556 3882 Fax: 0131 556 0279

Self Help Nottingham
Locally-based specialist self help development agency, although
undertakes some work on a national basis. Produces publications
and provides information, training and consultancy for self help
groups and professionals working in the field.
20 Pelham Rd, Sherwood Rise, Nottingham NG5 1AP
Tel: 0115 969 1212 (Monday-Friday, 9.00am-1.30pm)
Fax: 0115 960 2049

Sia
National development agency for the black voluntary sector.
Winchester House, 9 Cranmer Road, Kennington Park Road,
London SW9 6EJ Tel: 0171 735 9010 Fax: 0171 735 9011

Telephone Helplines Association
The aim of the Association is the assurance of the highest quality
response for all those seeking information, advice and help via
the telephone.
61 Grays Inn Road, London WC1X 8LT
Tel: 0171 242 0555 Fax: 0171 242 0699

Wales Council for Voluntary Action
Co-ordinates and develops voluntary action in Wales.
Llys Ifor, Crescent Road, Caerphilly, Mid-Glamorgan CF8 1XL
Tel: 01222 869224 Fax: 01222 860627

Books and training packs

Group work resources for use by self help groups

Doherty, Caroline; Firkin, Peter 1993 *Taking stock: issues for self
help groups. A training pack* London: NCVO ISBN 0 7199 1389 6

Douglas, Tom 1978 *Basic groupwork* London: Tavistock
ISBN 0 422 76320 9

Hill, Karen 1987 *Helping you helps me: a guide book for self-help
groups* Second edition   Ottawa, Ontario: Canadian Council on
Social Development ISBN 0 88810 372 7

Pinder, Caroline 1985 *Community start up: how to start a community group and keep it going* Cambridge: National Extension College / National Federation of Community Organisations ISBN 0 86082 572 8

Kindred, Michael 1987 *Once upon a group* Revised edition Southwell, Nottinghamshire: Michael Kindred ISBN 0 9512552 0 7

Lawyer, Linda 1989 *Changing places. From facilitator to mutual support: a guide for women's mutual support groups* Vancouver: Vancouver YWCA

Randall, Rosemary; Southgate, John; Tomlinson, Frances 1980 *Co-operative and community group dynamics . . . . or your meetings needn't be so appalling* London: Barefoot Books ISBN 0 9506273 1 3

Shahani, Vanessa 1995 *Group matters: a guide for self help support groups* Swindon: Health Matters

Town, Carol 1993 *Towards effective self-help: a group facilitation training manual* Hamilton, Ontario: Prevention Network of Hamilton-Wentworth

White, Barbara J.; Madara, Edward J. (eds.) 1995 *The self-help source book: finding and forming mutual aid self-help groups* Fifth edition Denville, N.J.: American Self-Help Clearinghouse ISBN 0 9634322 3 0

Available from SELF HELP NOTTINGHAM

Connect self help UK. A directory of locally based voluntary organisations offering support to self help groups 1997 Nottingham: Self Help Nottingham ISBN 0 9521031 17

Family Health Services Authority and The Self Help Team 1993 *"A self help group for your patient?" Guidelines for G.P. practices* Revised edition Nottingham: Self Help Team

Giving talks to professionals 1994 Revised edition Nottingham: Self Help Team

Listeners: guidelines for helpful listening 1991 Nottingham: Self Help Team

Starting off: information and ideas for new self help groups 1994 Revised edition Nottingham: Self Help Team

Wilson, Judy 1994 *Good links: guidelines on how self help groups can work with professionals* Nottingham: Self Help Team

Self help groups and professionals

Wilson, Judy 1995 *Two worlds: self help groups and professionals* Birmingham: British Association of Social Workers ISBN 1 873878 46 X

Wilson, Judy 1996 *How to work with self help groups: guidelines for professionals* Aldershot: Arena ISBN 1 85742 288 0

Theory and training materials designed to be used by professonals working with groups

Benson, Jarlath F. 1987 *Working more creatively with groups* London: Routledge ISBN 0 415 07587 4

Billingham, Kate 1990 *Learning together: a health resource pack for working with groups* Nottingham: Nottingham Comommunity Unit

Brandes, Donna; Phillips, Howard 1977 *Gamesters' handbook: 140 games for teachers and group leaders* London: Hutchinson ISBN 0 09 136421 3 (games and exercises to help people relax socially in group situations)

Douglas, Tom 1976 *Groupwork practice* London: Tavistock ISBN 0 422 74740 8

Henderson, P.; Foster, G. 1991 *Groupwork* Cambridge: National Extension College

Hunt, John 1989 *Introducing role play* Cumbria: Groundwork Group Development ISBN 1 869998 02 2 (practical ideas on how role play can contribute to group development)

Kirby, Andy (ed.) 1993 *Icebreakers* Aldershot, Hampshire: Gower ISBN 1 85904 044 6 (75 training exercises to encourage involvement of all group members)

Johnson, David W.; Johnson, Frank P. 1994 *Joining together: group theory and group skills* Fifth edition Boston: Allyn & Bacon ISBN 0 205 16017 4

Whitaker, Dorothy Stock 1985 *Using groups to help people* London: Routledge & Kegan Paul

Legal issues for community groups

Adirondack, Sandy; Taylor, James Sinclair 1997 *The voluntary sector legal handbook* Revised edition London: Directory of Social Change ISBN 1 873860 79

Forbes, Duncan; Hayes, Ruth; Reason, Jacki 1994 *Voluntary but not amateur: a guide to the law for voluntary organisations and community groups* 4th edition London: London Voluntary Service Council ISBN 1 872582 11 7

Ford, Kevin 1993 *The effective trustee. Part one: roles and responsibilities* London: Directory of Social Change ISBN1 873860 12 9

Ford, Kevin 1993 *The effective trustee. Part two: aims and resources* London: Directory of Social Change ISBN 1 873860 23 4

Ford, Kevin 1993 *The effective trustee. Part three: getting the work done* London: Directory of Social Change ISBN 1 873860 25 0

Kirkland, Kate 1995 *The good trustee guide: a resource organiser for members of governing bodies of unincorporated charities* London: NCVO ISBN 0 7199 1412 4

Directory

Voluntary Agencies Directory 1998 London: NCVO Publications. ISBN 0 719 91512 0 (Contains address of most national self help organisations)

Index

arena

How to Work with Self Help Groups

Guidelines for professionals

Judy Wilson

"Judy Wilson has become one of the world's leading authorities on self help groups. This book shows why. All readers from the complete beginner to the very experienced professional will benefit greatly from reading it." David Brandon, Chair, British Association of Social Workers.

Coping with loss, ill health and change are part of everyday life. The best support and information often comes from those who have already gone through a similar experience. Self help groups provide a different form of support when help from family, friends and professionals is not enough. Most professionals value self help groups, appreciating their special type of support and information. They want to work with them and are prepared to learn the best ways to do so. This handbook aims to help them to assess, extend or change how they work with self groups on a day to day basis.

Published by Arena, Gower House, Croft Road, Aldershot, Hants GU11 3HR, England.

Hardback £32.50 ISBN 1 85742 289 9
Paperback £14.95   ISBN 1 85742 288 0

SELF HELP NOTTINGHAM

20 Pelham Road, Sherwood Rise, Nottingham NG5 1AP
General enquiries (015) 969 969 1514. Fax (0115) 960 2049

PUBLICATIONS AND BOOKS FOR SALE

	Price	P & P
Directory of Self help groups in Nottingham and District (Updated annually)	£3.50	£1.00
Starting Off - Information and ideas for new self help groups - 2nd ed. 1994	£7.50	£0.40
A Self Help Group for your patient? Guidelines for GPs - 2nd ed. 1993	£1.00	£0.40
Giving Talks to Professionals - 2nd edition 1994	£1.60	£0.50
Connect Self Help UK - a directory of local voluntary organisations offering support to self hellp groups	£9.95	£1.75
Good Links - How self help groups can work with professionals. Judy Wilson.	£3.50	£0.50
How to work with Self Help Groups - Guidelines for Professionals. Judy Wilson Arena 1996	£14.95	£1.50

Coming soon:

Listening Skills
and
Keeping Going Pack
(new editions)

AMERICAN SELF-HELP CLEARINGHOUSE

Northwest Covenant Medical Center
25 Pocono Rd
Denville, New Jersey 07834-2995
Tel. +1(973)625-9565   Fax. +1(973)625-8848

The American Self-Help Clearinghouse developed from the New Jersey Self-Help Clearinghouse. The New Jersey Clearinghouse has assisted with the setting up of over 1050 new groups in the state since 1980 and provides a range of consultation, training and information services in New Jersey, available by phoning the number 800-FOR-M.A.S.H (Mutual Aid Self-Help).

Its work led to the provision of national services as the American Self-Help Clearinghouse in 1990. The American Clearinghouse provides information and referral on 973 625 3037 or TDD 973 625-9053 to callers across the USA. It provides some consultation if there is no group or support network for a particular problem in the USA.

It produces the Self-Help Sourcebook, containing an introduction to self-help groups, guidance on starting a group, advice to professionals working with self-help groups, advice for people operating telephone contact points for a group, a comprehensive listing of national self-help groups, networks and clearinghouses in the USA, and a full discussion on joining mutual help groups and networks on line through the Internet.

The Self-Help Source Book, 6th edition, 1998, is available from the Clearinghouse: Price $12 book rate in USA, $13 overseas surface, $16.00 overseas airmail. ISBN 0-9634322-7-3.

The present publication (**Self Help Groups: Getting started, keeping going**) can also be obtained in the USA from the Clearinghouse, price $ 17.50